The
Musical Comedy Murders
of
1940

The
Musical Comedy
Murders
of
1940

John Bishop

The Fireside Theatre
Garden City, New York

"for Bill Wildin, who made it happen."

Produced on Broadway by Bill Wildin, *The Musical Comedy Murders of 1940* was originally produced by the Circle Repertory Company, New York City on January 7, 1987. It was directed by the author with set design by David Potts, costumes by Jennifer von Mayrhauser, lighting by Mal Sturchio and Dennis Parichy. The production stage manager was Fred Reinglass. The cast was as follows:

HELSA WENZEL	Lily Knight
ELSA VON GROSSENKNUETEN	Ruby Holbrook
MICHAEL KELLY	Willie C. Carpenter
PATRICK O'REILLY	Nicholas Wyman
KEN DE LA MAIZE	Michael Ayr
NIKKI CRANDALL	Dorothy Cantwell
EDDIE MC CUEN	Kelly Connell
MARJORIE BAVERSTOCK	Pamela Dunlap
ROGER HOPEWELL	Richard Seff
BERNICE ROTH	Bobo Lewis

The production moved to the Longacre Theatre on Broadway on April 6, 1987.

The
Musical Comedy Murders
of
1940

CAST OF CHARACTERS

Helsa Wenzel
Elsa von Grossenknueten
Michael Kelly
Patrick O'Reilly
Ken de la Maize

Nikki Crandall
Eddie McCuen
Marjorie Baverstock
Roger Hopewell
Bernice Roth

The action of the play takes place in a mansion in Chappaqua, New York. The time is December 1940.

The setting is the library of the mansion. Entrances are: large, sliding double doors up center which lead to the main hall of the house, and French doors down right which lead to a garden.

There is a door to a walk-in closet up right center.

The walls of this room are lined with bookshelves, ceiling high. At three places in the room the bookshelves mask entrances to interior passageways in the house. One of these entrances is up left center. Here a section of the bookcase revolves to reveal the passageway.

Another passage is behind a sliding bookcase up right. And yet another behind a sliding bookcase down left.

As for set dressing, stage left is a desk and two chairs. Down left another chair. There is a bar built into bookcases stage right. Right center a piano and bench. Center stage, over the doorway hangs a portrait of a German general, circa 1870. Crossed sabers hang beneath it.

When the play opens, it is midnight—naturally.

Act One

ACT ONE

(A maid, HELSA, enters carrying a serving tray with teapot and two cups. She places tray on desk, turns on desk lamp, straightens pillow on wing chair down left. From stage right, behind the drapes, we hear a voice.)

VOICE: Helsa, you forgot the sugar. *(HELSA stops, surprised)* Helsa!

(HELSA crosses to drapes, holds out hand tentatively to touch drapes. A FIGURE dressed entirely in black leaps out and stabs her to death. The FIGURE then attempts to stuff her body behind the drapes . . . but first an arm, then a leg, and, as the FIGURE stuffs the leg under the drapes, finally the entire torso and head pop out. In frustration the FIGURE looks around the room, sees the closet, and, picking her up in a fireman's carry, stuffs her inside. FIGURE hears someone approaching and runs and hides behind drapes. ELSA and SGT. KELLY enter. She is an attractive middle-aged woman. He is a large black man wearing a trench coat and carrying a makeup kit.)

ELSA: And this is the library. Here's the room where our adventure will begin.

KELLY: Our what?

ELSA: *(Beside herself with excitement)* The game's afoot, eh, Sergeant?

KELLY: Are you sure you understand exactly what we're doin' here?

ELSA: Of course. As I told your captain yesterday, I am not unfamiliar with the wiles and artifices of police work.

KELLY: Well, we're not doin' wiles or artifices here, ma'am. We're settin' up a killer and . . .

ELSA: Quite, and since we have an early day tomorrow, we'd best have our Ovaltine and go to bed. Oh dear, Helsa has forgotten the sugar.

KELLY: Not on my account.

ELSA: You don't take sugar?

KELLY: I don't take Ovaltine.

ELSA: If it's good enough for Orphan Annie, Sergeant . . .

(Picks up list from desk and crosses to KELLY*)*

Here is a list of the people you are picking up in the morning. At nine-thirty A.M. in front of the Brill Building, a Mr. Eddie McCuen. Mr. McCuen is a struggling young comedian. The Brill Building is—

KELLY: Yeah, I know where it is.

ELSA: Of course you do. Then Miss Baverstock will be at her apartment at 230 East Fiftieth. Oh—Mr. McCuen is, I am given to understand, an incredibly struggling young comedian. Perhaps, to spare Miss Baverstock, he'd best ride up front with you.

KELLY: Swell.

ELSA: Then, at a house on East Ninety-second Street you are to pick up an actor named Patrick O'Reilly. Mr. O'Reilly is an Irish tenor.

KELLY: You told this Miss Baverstock you had a new chauffeur?

ELSA: I made up some story, yes. The others arrive by car and train. I do hope they make their connections.

(She crosses toward radio)

KELLY: Snow's supposed to stop by midnight.

(ELSA *has turned on the radio. We hear* "Jeanie with the Light Brown Hair")

ELSA: I wish they'd settle whatever it is they're striking about. I'm sick of Stephen Foster.

(She dials a weather report)

RADIO (VO): . . . and still falling all along the Eastern seaboard. What had been originally estimated as two inches has already doubled that with no end in sight . . .

KELLY: I hope this won't scare off our people.

ELSA: What?

(She turns radio down)

KELLY: I said, I hope this won't scare off our people.

ELSA: My dear, these are actors, producer, director, composer, lyricist, coming to get my money for their Broadway show. Nothing short of the end of the world will stop them.

KELLY: If this is gonna work, you've got to say the speech exactly like we rehearsed it. And you're going to be able to pull off your end of this okay?

ELSA: Espionage is in my blood, Sergeant. I won't fail you.

(She has crossed to desk and picked up makeup kit)

Poor Bebe's Deco makeup kit. Being *au courant* was so important to her. And now . . . she is anything but.

KELLY: *(Handing her a small notebook)* Here.

ELSA: Ahh, yes. That which may reveal a murderer.

(Puts notebook in makeup kit)

Oh, Sergeant, this is going to be a grand adventure, isn't it?

(Puts kit in desk drawer, and picks up a list)

And I've planned a perfectly grand menu for the occasion. To begin, a tureen of December fruit, followed by lobster on dill, and . . .

KELLY: Yeah, well since my first adventure will be drivin' through a snowstorm tomorrow, I better get some sleep.

ELSA: Come, I'll show you to your room.

(She turns off lamp on desk. As they go to door . . .)

I must admit, you are something of a surprise to me, Sergeant. I had thought all New York City policemen to be Irish.

KELLY: We are.

(She turns off the lights in the room. They exit. The FIGURE steps out from behind the drapes, begins to cross the stage, hears something on the radio, goes back, turns it up and listens.)

RADIO (VO): . . . Nor the Federal Bureau of Investigation would confirm these rumors. The Nazi submarine is believed to have landed these men on the shore off Long Island earlier this month. With the discovery of the body of Franz Becker, knifed to death in the back of a restaurant in the Yorkville section of Manhattan, it is now believed that only one, possibly the leader, of the saboteurs is still at large. In other news, The British Eighth Army announced success today in North Africa near Sidi Barrani . . .

(FIGURE turns radio off . . . crosses to desk. Takes out makeup kit and removes notebook. FIGURE leafs through it quickly . . . then throws it back in kit, and puts kit back in desk drawer.

FIGURE *stands tapping knife as he thinks. An owl is heard outside. Lights fade to black.*

A car gunning its motor, obviously stuck in the snow, is heard as the lights come up. HELSA *enters, looks around the room, and starts to cross to the French doors.* ELSA, *bundled in furs, enters.)*

ELSA: Helsa, there seems to be a taxi stuck in the drive. I'm going down with a shovel. And the bar needs condiments. Will you see to it?

HELSA: *Ja, gnädige Frau.*

ELSA: *Gnädige Frau?* A bit formal this morning, aren't we? Oh, I think I know. Little Helsa is curious about my overnight guest, isn't she?

HELSA: *Nein.*

ELSA: Not even curious which bedroom he slept in?

(Laughs and attempts to kiss her. HELSA *turns her head)*

Oh, don't worry, you're still the princess here. Now, to the day. There will be seven for lunch, four for dinner. I want you at your most efficient today, Helsa. I'm not at liberty to tell you why, but this day will add a bone-chilling chapter to the von Grossenknueten annals.

(As she goes, points to Ovaltine tray)

Clear that also, will you?

(She exits center. HELSA *turns to the French doors.* O'REILLY *stands outside. She starts . . . then opens doors.)*

O'REILLY: Thank you, thank you. Sure and we're after bein' stuck down on the road at the bottom of your driveway, wouldn't you know.

HELSA: *Ja,* I hear the car.

O'REILLY: No, that's another car. We can't even get up the hill. I'm Patrick O'Reilly.

(He takes off his hat to reveal a close-cropped blond head. He is a large, rather sinister man with a saber scar across his left cheek.)

I'm one of the actors. I thought I'd be after comin' up to see if I could borrow a shovel. *(He pronounces it "shivel")*

HELSA: Shivel? Oh . . . Fräulein von Grossenknueten is using it right now. May I take your coat?

O'REILLY: I may as well go back down, then, and see what I can do.

(He crosses to French doors)

HELSA: You are Irish, Mr. O'Reilly?

O'REILLY: As Paddy's cow. And you . . . are Scandinavian?

HELSA: I am German.

O'REILLY: Are you now?

HELSA: A refugee. Fräulein von Grossenknueten gave me refuge here four years ago.

O'REILLY: Did she now?

HELSA: From the Nazis.

O'REILLY: The Nazis, was it?

HELSA: Swine that they are!

O'REILLY: *(After a beat)* I see.

(Beat) Well . . . it's been most interestin' meetin' you, Miss—?

HELSA: Wenzel. Helsa Wenzel.

O'REILLY: Wenzel, yes.

(Turns to go. Stops)

Faith and begorrah, but isn't there a very famous German cabaret entertainer named Wenzel? At the Tivoli, I believe.

HELSA: You are familiar with German cabaret entertainers?

O'REILLY: Well, it's after bein' my business now, isn't it? Dieter Wenzel, isn't that his name?

HELSA: I never paid much attention to the cabarets.

(From the hallway, center, we hear voices. ELSA *enters followed by* KEN DE LA MAIZE *and* NIKKI CRANDALL. KEN *is a handsome man in his mid-forties. His clothes and tan are Hollywood.* NIKKI *is a beautiful young woman in her twenties. She occasionally wears glasses, but it makes not a whit of difference to her beauty. She is carrying a shoulder bag, and an envelope with lead sheets.)*

ELSA: This is the library. We'll hold the audition here, Ken.

(KEN *looks around the room, crosses to wing chair, and moves it a few inches.)*

Director at work.

(KEN *moves the chair back a few inches)*

You can move it around any way you like.

KEN: It's perfect.

ELSA: *(Turning to* O'REILLY*)* Hello. I'm Elsa von Grossenknueten.

O'REILLY: *(Clicking his heels)* I'm Patrick O'Reilly. Our group is stuck down below. I came up for a shivel.

ELSA: A shivel?

HELSA: *(Exiting with tray of Ovaltine)* A shovel.

ELSA: Oh, shovel, of course! Well, it's right outside the door.

(Introducing others)

This is Miss Nikki . . . ahh . . .

NIKKI: Crandall.

ELSA: And this is Ken de la Maize, your director.

O'REILLY: Pleased to meet you, I'm sure. And now, I'll be after gettin' that shivel. *(He crosses to door)*

ELSA: I'll go with you.

O'REILLY: It's after bein' down to the bottom of the hill, Miss. And the snow is as steep as the cliffs of Killarney.

ELSA: I am of solid Bavarian stock, Mr. O'Reilly. Snow is in my blood.

KEN: But not in your heart, dear Elsa.

(To NIKKI*)*

This lady is the most generous patron of our art alive today.

ELSA: Am I, Ken?

KEN: Without you, Elsa, there wouldn't be more than thirty or forty shows on the Great White Way. She backed twelve last season.

(HELSA *enters with the condiments and goes to the bar*)

ELSA: Well, I do like to dabble. Now Ken, suppose you mix you and Miss Crandall a drink. Helsa will take your luggage to your room. Northwest guest room, Helsa.

(HELSA *exits*)

Roger and Bernice will be down as soon as they thaw out. Marjorie is trudging up the hill. Soon we'll all be together once more, won't we, Ken?

KEN: Yes. It'll be good to see Roger and Bernice again.

ELSA: All . . . together, right, Ken?

KEN: *(A bit bewildered by her attitude)* Yes.

ELSA: *(Mood changing)* And when I come back, I want to hear all about Hollywood. What it's like.

KEN: Just dump the garment district in the middle of an orange grove. That's Hollywood.

ELSA: *(As she goes)* How picturesque!

(O'REILLY *follows her out*)

KEN: Of course there is an ocean somewhere.

NIKKI: You never saw the ocean?

KEN: Certainly I saw the ocean. I was at a party in Santa Monica one night and someone pulled open the drapes. Drink?

NIKKI: No, thank you.

KEN: You were about to tell me in the cab which show you were with in Washington.

NIKKI: *Du Barry.*

KEN: You know Bob, then.

NIKKI: Bob?

KEN: Bob Alton. The choreographer.

NIKKI: This was the road company. Jimmy Arnemann staged it.

KEN: Oh. And you closed in Washington?

NIKKI: No, I left the show in Washington.

KEN: Not to come up here for a backer's audition, I hope?

NIKKI: Oh no, I've got—other things on the fire.

KEN: And you're a singer/dancer?

NIKKI: Dancer, mostly.

KEN: Yes, I kind of thought that when I watched you get off the train.

NIKKI: I walk like a duck, you mean?

KEN: No, you tripped over your suitcase.

NIKKI: Sure sign.

KEN: And with whom did you study dance?

NIKKI: Well, see, I'm from Chicago . . .

KEN: I know Chicago quite well.

NIKKI: Actually south of there. You know Kankakee?

KEN: I'm afraid not.

NIKKI: I studied there with Natasha Dubrovitska.

KEN: I see.

NIKKI: *(Changing subject)* Jeepers, this is a swell house, isn't it?

KEN: Yes.

NIKKI: I'll bet they have some swell houses in Hollywood.

KEN: Ostentatious, but . . . "swell," yes.

NIKKI: You live out there?

KEN: I'm hoping this enterprise will bring me back to New York.

NIKKI: You're not working on any movies now?

KEN: I've just finished a picture. *Moonlight in Rio.*

NIKKI: *Moonlight in Rio?* You shot a movie in Brazil?

KEN: No, I shot it in Culver City. Except for the beach. The beach I shot in Oxnard.

NIKKI: Who's in it?

KEN: Alice Faye, Dick Powell, Phil Silvers, Ann Miller, Patsy Kelly, George Brent, Lauritz Melchior, Jascha Heifetz, and Borrah Minevitch.

NIKKI: Oh sure, I saw that.

KEN: You probably did; but this one hasn't been released yet.

NIKKI: Oh.

KEN: Ahhhh, it's good . . . good to be back.

NIKKI: New York?

KEN: The theater. That event as ancient as man and as mysterious and inspiring as the nature man once sought to imitate or appease in his earliest rituals . . . rituals we now call—the theater. Not moving pictures, but life. Life distilled to a pure clear ring of truth. Never forget that. It is your heritage.

NIKKI: I guess. But I've only done musical comedy.

KEN: Yes. Well, if you'll excuse me, I'm going to take my sherry upstairs and into the bathtub. Get rid of some of the Union Pacific Railroad I've brought with me.

NIKKI: Sure, go ahead. I want to look over the lead sheets anyway.

(She drops her purse on piano. It makes a very loud thud. She smiles at KEN)

KEN: See you later.

(He exits center. NIKKI takes lead sheets from envelope. A man appears outside the French doors and raps "Shave and a haircut —two bits" on the glass. He is EDDIE MCCUEN, a young, energetic man in his late twenties. NIKKI crosses and opens the door. Mid swirling snow, EDDIE steps in.)

EDDIE: Hi. I'm Admiral Byrd. Am I lost? This is the North Pole? Boy, what a blizzard! I passed four penguins on my way up here. One of them was wearing a polar bear.

(He snaps fingers, à la rim shot)

Only kidding. I'm Eddie McCuen. This your place?

NIKKI: No, I'm Nikki Crandall. Miss von Grossenknueten just went down the hill to help some people who are stuck.

EDDIE: That's us. And a taxi ahead of us and a car behind us. They'll never make it up the hill. I decided to hoof it. *(He crosses center)*

NIKKI: Your boots! The oriental.

EDDIE: *(Jumps off carpet)* Oh, yeah—sorry.

(Sits on piano bench to remove galoshes)

You here for the audition?

NIKKI: Yes.

EDDIE: You write it or . . . ?

NIKKI: I'm an actress.

EDDIE: Great. Guess we'll be working together.

NIKKI: You're an actor?

EDDIE: Well, I'm a comedian, actually. You see *Hellzapoppin'*?

NIKKI: Are you in it?

EDDIE: I had a couple of bits, yeah. I just left it a month ago. Doin' some radio.

(Picking up his coat, hat, and galoshes, he crosses stage toward center door. Sees closet.)

This the closet?

(EDDIE opens the closet door which swings onstage and toward right. Just as he does this, NIKKI speaks so that EDDIE turns back to her. He therefore is not looking into closet and NIKKI is looking down at lead sheets, which is a good thing, because in the closet stiffly stands a dead HELSA WENZEL, clothed only in bra and panties. She begins falling forward.)

NIKKI: The coat closet is outside in the hall.

EDDIE: Oh.

(He closes the door, stopping HELSA's *fall. There is a thud on the door, which they don't hear.)*

Out here?

(Pointing to upstage door)

NIKKI: Yes.

*(*EDDIE *exits.* NIKKI *is looking at sheet music)*

> "Pardon me, is that my heart,
> On my sleeve while we're apart?"

(After a moment EDDIE *returns and crosses to her.)*

EDDIE: Oh, you've got music.

NIKKI: Yeah, didn't they send you some?

EDDIE: I only got the gig yesterday. Some other guy got sick. My agent asked me, can I sing. Sure, I say—always say "yes," one of my rules. No matter what they ask, yes. This morning a limo picks me up, parks me in front with the chauffeur. Then we pick up a dame and a mug in Yorkville. What a trip! Driving in a snowstorm. I can't see a thing so I don't know how the driver can. And on top of that he's deaf.

NIKKI: Deaf?

EDDIE: Had to be. I did forty minutes of my best stuff . . . he don't crack a smile.

(Looking at music)

"White House Merry-Go-Round."

NIKKI: Nice tune.

EDDIE: By Roger Hopewell and Bernice Roth. Hopewell and Roth! Hey, is this gonna be one of their shows?

NIKKI: Guess so.

EDDIE: Hot dog!

NIKKI: You don't get any better than that.

EDDIE: What a break! They got a string of hits. I think except for *Manhattan Holiday* they've never had a flop. What's the other music? Is there a number for a comic?

NIKKI: I don't know, but I'm sure Mr. de la Maize will assign parts.

EDDIE: Ken de la Maize? He's here too? He's the director? Hot dog!

NIKKI: Yes. You didn't know that?

EDDIE: I don't know anything except I'm getting twenty-five bucks to do a backers' audition for some dame named von Grossen-somethin'.

NIKKI: Knueten.

EDDIE: No, thanks. I just had a Danish. *(He does his finger snap)*

NIKKI: That's her name: von Grossenknueten.

EDDIE: Hey, that was a joke. I'm a comic, remember?

NIKKI: I'll try.

EDDIE: Boy, this is the opportunity of a lifetime. To be in at the start of a hit show. I guess they're lookin' for a producer.

NIKKI: As I understand it, they've got a producer. They want an angel.

EDDIE: Who's the producer?

NIKKI: Marjorie Baverstock.

EDDIE: Hot dog! Marjorie Baverstock! Oh my gosh!

(A look of horror on his face, he runs out)

NIKKI: She was probably the woman in your car. Was she wearing mink?

(But EDDIE has dashed out of the room. In a moment he runs back in carrying hat, coat, scarf, and galoshes, and struggling to get them on as he moves to the French doors.)

You're going back out?

EDDIE: I'm going back, period. To New York City.

NIKKI: What?

EDDIE: C'mon, grab your coat. *(Stops to explain to her)* It's the same people—*Manhattan Holiday*. The same creative team.

NIKKI: So they had a dud. That scares you back to New York?

EDDIE: No, the Stage Door Slasher scares me back to New York. Get your coat!

NIKKI: The who?

EDDIE: Where ya been? The Stage Door Slasher! Two years ago? Three women murdered. All chorus girls. All in *Manhattan Holiday*.

NIKKI: Oh yeah, now I remember reading something. See, I was on the road and . . .

EDDIE: They had to close the show. The chorus wouldn't come to work until they caught the Slasher. And lady, they never caught him. So let's hit the breeze!

NIKKI: If he only killed women, what are you so worried about?

EDDIE: How do I know he hasn't changed his preferences? C'mon!

NIKKI: What makes you think the killer would be here? There are no chorus girls here . . .

(They look at each other)

. . . wait a minute, I'll get my coat.

(She crosses to door . . . stops)

Oh, this is silly. That was two years ago. And the only similarity is the creative team. Anyhow, you'll never get back to New York in this weather. Look how thick the snow is falling. It's a dark, sunless day. For all you know, the killer may be stranded out there, hidden by the snow . . . waiting . . . and it's just going to get darker and darker and—

EDDIE: You can stop before you get to Dracula's entrance, okay? C'mon get your coat. I'll leave her a note.

(Crosses to desk for pen)

I'll take my chances outside. Why, there must be twenty-five rooms in this joint and the Slasher could be hiding in any of them. And that don't count the closets.

(By moving the penholder, he has caused the revolving book-case up left to half-open.)

NIKKI: My gosh!

EDDIE: What?

(Sees bookcase. Starts to run to French doors. NIKKI runs to the bookcase.)

NIKKI: A secret passage!

EDDIE: Let's get out of here!

NIKKI: Let's take a look!

EDDIE: My gosh, they do exist!

NIKKI: Who do?

EDDIE: I thought it was only in movies where whenever there's a lunatic killer loose and killin' everybody and his brother, somebody, usually a dame, hears a noise in the hen house and goes out in the pitch-black night to investigate.

NIKKI: And did you ever notice, in those same movies there's always a big strong hero who's not afraid of the dark?

EDDIE: I'm a comic, remember? The dark definitely scares us. It's part of our training.

(Through the center door enter ELSA, O'REILLY, and MARJORIE BAVERSTOCK. MARJORIE is anywhere from thirty-five to sixty years of age. She is quite expensively dressed and carries herself like royalty.)

ELSA: Ah, you must be Mr. McCuen, since you're the only one unaccounted for. I'm your hostess, Elsa von Grossenknueten. And of course you know Miss Baverstock and Mr. O'Reilly, since you rode up with them.

MARJORIE: Hardly know, Elsa, as Mr. McCuen was up front with your driver. I didn't get an opportunity to tell you, Mr. McCuen, that I think it's simply divoon of you to fill in at the last moment like this.

EDDIE: Well thanks, but I—

ELSA: And this is Miss Crandall. Nikki darling, I don't believe you've met Miss Baverstock.

(As they exchange "hellos," ELSA notices EDDIE is wearing his coat and one boot.)

Do you . . . ah . . . have a cold, Mr. McCuen?

EDDIE: No, see, there's been a hitch. I got my dates mixed and I'm due back in New York.

ELSA: Oh dear, when?

EDDIE: *(Looking at watch)* Well, it would be . . . right now.

ELSA: Really? But my goodness, I don't know how you'll get there. Perhaps it's skipped your attention, but we're having a blizzard.

EDDIE: I know, but—

MARJORIE: Well I know I, for one, would be quite sorry to see you go. I've been hearing such good things about your work. And of course Ken de la Maize, who is directing the audition, is so very big in Hollywood these days. Is Hollywood in your future?

EDDIE: *(Crossing to NIKKI)* Come on, let's get to work.

NIKKI: What about the Slasher?

EDDIE: Let him get his own agent.

MARJORIE: Elsa, I can't wait for you to hear the show. It's divoon, simply divoon. And I have a budget all worked out. Even down to the opening night party. We'll hold it at Sardi's, naturally, and if we charge the actors just a teensy cover charge, we'll break even.

(Seeing back of revolving bookcase)

Elsa, are you redecorating?

ELSA: *(She moves the penholder, and the bookcase swings open)*
Oh my, the bookcase has been turned. Did someone move
the penholder?

EDDIE: Oh, I guess I did that.

MARJORIE: A secret passage, Elsa? Where does it lead?

ELSA: To other passages. The house is laced with them.

MARJORIE: My goodness, Nancy Drew would be in seventh
heaven here, wouldn't she? You never told me about this,
Elsa, never!

ELSA: They're nothing, Marjorie. Just your average, ordinary,
everyday secret passageways.

*(She moves the penholder again, and the revolve goes to its
original position)*

MARJORIE: Was this a stop on the Underground Railway or
something?

ELSA: No.

MARJORIE: Then why . . . ?

ELSA: My father, who built this house, was Baron Wilhelm von
Grossenknueten.

O'REILLY: Ahhh, yes.

ELSA: You've heard of him?

O'REILLY: Well . . . aah, wasn't there a motion picture about
him? With Erich von Stroheim? Or am I thinkin' of someone
else?

ELSA: Someone else. Though he was a legend, there has been no motion picture on him.

O'REILLY: Obviously I have him mixed up.

ELSA: This house was built by him when he left Germany at the end of the war.

MARJORIE: He was a general?

ELSA: He was the Kaiser's chief of espionage and the most brilliant intelligence mind in European history.

NIKKI: He was a spy?

ELSA: You've perhaps heard of the Dreyfuss papers? The Colonel Redl letter? The Kruger telegram? The Von Moltke note? The Hotzendorff paragraph? The Holstein sentence? The Von Emmich preposition? The . . .

MARJORIE: But why the secret passages?

ELSA: It was the . . . only way he could leave the room.

(KEN *enters*)

KEN: Is all our company met?

MARJORIE: Ken darling! How divoon!

KEN: Marjorie, honey.

MARJORIE: Kids, this is Ken de la Maize, your director. Whom haven't you met, Ken?

EDDIE: Hi, I'm Eddie McCuen. I just did *Hellzapoppin'* and—

KEN: Eddie. We'll go to work shortly, but—

(HELSA *enters*)

HELSA: Excuse me, *gnädige Frau,* but I cannot find the meat cleaver.

ELSA: You need a meat cleaver?

HELSA: For the hors d'oeuvres, *ja.*

ELSA: Well . . . if you need it.

(Starting out)

My home is yours, everyone. Make yourselves comfortable. I'll be right back. You're sure you mean a meat cleaver, Helsa?

HELSA: *Ja wohl.*

(ELSA *and* HELSA *exit*)

MARJORIE: *(Crossing to penholder)* Ken darling, look.

(She moves penholder, and the bookcase opens and closes)

A secret passage.

KEN: So it is. Very like the one I just used in *The Circular Staircase,* with Paulette Goddard, Laird Cregar, Judith Anderson, Lionel Atwill, George Sanders, Peter Lorre, and John Carradine.

MARJORIE: I saw it, Ken, and it was some of your best work.

KEN: It hasn't been released yet. Now, cast, as I was saying, we will go to work shortly. But let me remind you that although this is only a backers' audition for an audience of one, it is still theater. So, any questions of character or interpretation you have . . . bring them out. Theater is nothing more or less than life distilled to the pure, clear ring of truth. A ritual as old as—

(ROGER *enters, carrying a portfolio of sheet music*)

ROGER: Quick, someone, a martini—I am in danger of frostbite.

MARJORIE: Roger darling! You look divoon! Simply divoon!

ROGER: Marjorie sweetheart, love your new word.

MARJORIE: Let me introduce. Actors, this is Roger Hopewell. They're to do your music, Roger. Miss Crandall, Mr. McCuen, Mr. O'Reilly.

ROGER: *(To* O'REILLY*)* Your eyes are very blue.

MARJORIE: Perhaps I will have a drink now. It makes it so much easier to excuse licentious behavior.

ROGER: I was not being licentious, Marjorie. A trifle libidinous perhaps. A bit lascivious. But not licentious.

MARJORIE: What's the difference?

KEN: The placement of the tongue, I imagine.

ROGER: Ken! I didn't see you. How wonderful to be working with you again. I was saying to Bernice on the way here, now our script will have distilled truth, and clean rings, and new spark plugs, and all those wonderful things Ken does.

(Seeing EDDIE*)*

And you are the comic.

EDDIE: Right. You've seen me work?

ROGER: No. I merely assumed that was why you were only wearing one overshoe.

EDDIE: My gosh, forgot all about it. *(Sits on piano bench and removes it)*

ROGER: *(Crossing to bar)* I must have that martini.

MARJORIE: *(Above piano, with martini shaker)* How about our performers? Dare you have a drink before attempting to entice Elsa out of her money?

NIKKI: No, thank you.   O'REILLY: Not right now, thanks.

EDDIE: I wouldn't mind a shot of bourbon, if you've got it.

(BERNICE ROTH *enters. She is forty to fifty, dresses like a gypsy dancer. Her arms are piled with bracelets which rattle every time she moves.)*

BERNICE: Hi, gang.

MARJORIE: *(Rushing to embrace her)* Bernice, darling.

KEN: Bernice, you're looking wonderful.

(BERNICE, *upon hearing her name, turns to go to* KEN, *and* MARJORIE *misses her, almost kissing the bookcase instead)*

BERNICE: *(To* KEN) Missed ya, kid.

KEN: You've added a bracelet, I see.

MARJORIE: Have a drink with us, Bernice. I'm having a teeny martooni.

BERNICE: In that case I'll have a huge Manhootan.

ROGER: With a cherry?

BERNICE: Be realistic, Roger.

MARJORIE: This, cast, is Bernice Roth, the librettist.

(To BERNICE*)*

Your cast.

ROGER: *(Handing* MARJORIE *martini)* Martini time!

BERNICE: Hi, gang. Sorry I'm late getting downstairs, but the storm froze the lock on my overnight case and I've been upstairs heating it with a candle.

MARJORIE: Heating the lock?

BERNICE: And the candle kept dripping wax on the rug so I moved into the closet and set something on fire.

MARJORIE: Set what on fire?

BERNICE: Well, see, I don't know, 'cause whatever it was burned up. Then the maid comes in while I'm kneeling on the floor in the closet under this raging fire and wants to know if I'm Haitian!

(Noticing O'REILLY*)*

Your eyes are very blue.

EDDIE: *(To* NIKKI*)* Ain't it somethin' to be with all these famous people?

NIKKI: I guess so.

*(*HELSA *enters with more ice for the bar. She then picks up* EDDIE*'s galoshes, coat, hat, etc., all the while exchanging glances with* O'REILLY. EDDIE *notices them looking at each other.)*

ROGER: *(To* KEN*)* Ken, love your tan.

KEN: It only cost one soul.

ROGER: May cost us ours. Bernice and I have been asked to do a motion picture later this year. You know who Abbott and Costello are?

KEN: Those two guys in the Bobby Clark thing?

EDDIE: *Streets of Paris.*

ROGER: *Streets of Paris.* Well, Universal has signed them and we've been approached about some songs.

MARJORIE: That reminds me. The lead dancer from that show. The boy—Grover Champion—

EDDIE: Gower Champion.

MARJORIE: We should think about him. I know you're only in first draft, Bernice, but think about taking that long, long, loooong section where the sailor is telling the girl how beautiful she is and making it a ballet.

BERNICE: I didn't think that section was all that long.

ROGER: Ever notice, in Bernice's writing, every time someone tells a woman how beautiful she is, the scene goes on forever.

BERNICE: That comes from understanding romance, Roger. A subject you are somewhat hazy on.

ROGER: That comes from writing in front of that smoked mirror you've got over your desk, is what it comes from.

KEN: Come on, kids, let's get to work.

(ELSA *enters*)

ELSA: Ahhh, we are all together once more, are we not? All together. And are we all comfortable?

ROGER: We're fine, Elsa.

KEN: We're about to start rehearsal, Elsa.

ELSA: *(Crossing to French doors)* Does anyone need a refill?

BERNICE: Sure. *(She drains her glass)*

ELSA: Heavens, how dark it's getting, and it's only just past one. Wonderful! *(She chuckles)* The snow just won't stop, will it? What are you having, Bernice?

BERNICE: What's closest?

(HELSA enters)

HELSA: Excuse me, *gnädige Frau,* but your cook called and is snowed in.

ELSA: *(Slamming down her glass)* Drat!

(Softening)

Well, there's nothing for it but I shall go in the kitchen and whip up a quick lunch. We don't want you hungry for the big show, do we?

(Laughs and heads for door)

Come Helsa, let's see if we remember how to do sauerbraten.

(ELSA and HELSA exit)

ROGER: Sauerbraten?

MARJORIE: How inspired! She's chosen a dish, that even if she ruined, no one could tell the difference.

KEN: I suggest we get started with rehearsals, since that is why we're here.

ROGER: Is it?

(Everyone looks at him)

Hasn't anyone wondered why this particular creative group has been gathered in this particular house?

MARJORIE: A backers' audition.

ROGER: Featuring the team whose last effort was *Manhattan Holiday*. The show during which one Bebe McAllister, Elsa's . . . "friend" . . . was murdered.

(Beat)

Another drink, Ken? You look as though you need one.

KEN: It's just the memory of that horrible time. I had hoped it was forgotten.

ROGER: Obviously it isn't. Though Elsa is . . . eccentric, though she walks through life thinking she's Gale Sondergaard . . . her behavior today strikes me as more batty than usual.

MARJORIE: If that's possible.

ROGER: And I believe we have been gathered for a dual purpose.

KEN: Which is?

ROGER: She wants to observe us . . . together.

KEN: To what end?

O'REILLY: Excuse me, but who was murdered?

EDDIE: Were you in New York two years ago?

O'REILLY: Two years ago I was off visitin' me old mither in County Cork.

EDDIE: You were visiting a "mither"? *(To* NIKKI) What's a "mither"?

NIKKI: Mother.

KEN: Someone killed three members of our dancing chorus.

O'REILLY: And this killer was a member of the show?

KEN: We don't know.

ROGER: Of course we know. We play New Haven, a murder. Boston, a murder. Philadelphia . . .

ALL: Terrible reviews.

ROGER: And a murder closes us in New York. Someone with the show, Ken.

EDDIE: *(To* NIKKI) See, I told you!

O'REILLY: And you suspect the killer is in this house?

ROGER: Yes.

O'REILLY: *(Laughs)* I am sorry, but you're not after knowin' much about murderers. They may occasionally be drawn back to the scene of the crime. But they never—once they are free and away—never would intentionally associate themselves with anyone who could possibly have reason to suspect them.

EDDIE: Hey, how do you know so much about murderers?

O'REILLY: My old fither and me fither's fither, God rest their souls, were police officers.

BERNICE: And you're a tenor?

ROGER: I still think that's why we've been gathered here.

O'REILLY: Sounds like a parlor game, Mr. Hopewell. Murder is never so interestin'. In real life it is sudden, and filled with rage. Quite emotional. Quite messy. No secret passages. Just blood-soaked carpets.

(HELSA, *who has obviously been listening just outside the door, in the hall, enters with a tray of hors d'oeuvres and glances quickly in the direction of the French doors.* O'REILLY *notices her looking)*

HELSA: What blood-soaked carpet?

(All look at her)

Excuse me, I thought I heard something about a blood-soaked carpet.

MARJORIE: We were talking about real life, Helsa. Though God knows why, since we're here to do a musical comedy.

(O'REILLY *has walked to French doors, looking at carpet.)*

HELSA: Fräulein von Grossenknueten has asked me to tell you, lunch will be served in about thirty minutes. In the meantime, there are hors d'oeuvres.

KEN: I suggest we get started with the rehearsal. Which, Roger, is the only reason we are gathered here.

ROGER: Just thought it worth mentioning.

MARJORIE: Well, if you believe there to be a killer loose, best not to stand in front of the bookcase. It's a secret passage.

(She pushes the penholder and the bookcase opens and closes)

ROGER: Good heavens!

KEN: Are we going to work or shall we all get in pajamas and continue to tell ghost stories? Actors, over here. *(Indicating piano curve)* Bernice and Roger at the piano.

HELSA: *(Who has been passing tray)* I'm sorry there is no bratwurst, Mr. O'Reilly, since you are so interested in things German.

(She leaves tray on the piano and exits)

KEN: Bernice, have you—Bernice?

BERNICE: *(Has moved to the center chair, and is staring at the bookcase that just moved)* Hmmm?

KEN: Have you decided how much of the book we are going to do?

BERNICE: What?

KEN: The book.

MARJORIE: Bernice!

BERNICE: What?

MARJORIE: Has this silliness of Roger's frightened you?

BERNICE: Oh no, of course not. I was just thinking. We have nothing to be afraid of here. My God, we're warm and cozy in a lovely, old, kinda weird house . . . with secret passages, and blood-soaked carpets, and sorta isolated by a snowstorm.

(ELSA enters)

ELSA: I'm afraid I have a rather troubling announcement. I hope none of you have to reach New York this afternoon because the phone seems to have gone dead.

BERNICE: *(Still matter-of-fact)* and the phone seems to have gone dead . . .

(Total panic)

Help! We're all going to be murdered! Help!

(BERNICE *runs to the French doors in a panic.* KEN, ROGER, *and* MARJORIE *bring her back to the chair and try to calm her down*)

KEN: Wait, Bernice, wait, there's nothing to be afraid of!	MARJORIE: Bernice, darling, please!	ROGER: Bernice, for heaven's sake, calm down!

EDDIE: *(Brings* NIKKI *down right)* Know something?

NIKKI: What?

EDDIE: I think she's got a point.

(As NIKKI *looks at* EDDIE *the lights fade to black.*

A pause . . . then music begins. ROGER *is playing and singing along with* EDDIE, NIKKI, *and* O'REILLY. BERNICE *is by the bar.* MARJORIE *is seated in wing chair down left. They are singing* White House Merry-Go-Round)

> Hopkins still in though out
> Farley has lost his clout
> you've got to know the way
> who's got whose ear today.
>
> Ickes and Cordell Hull
> won't even take your call
> 'less you're inside of the,
> takin' a ride on the,
> White House
> merry-go-round.

MARJORIE: *(Applauding and gushing)* I love it so far and so will Elsa. The tunes . . . the lyrics . . . divoon! Simply divoon!

KEN: Let's get on to the second act. It's already four and Elsa wants to see this before dinner.

Nicholas Wyman, Ruby Holbrook and Lily Knight

l. to r.-Nicholas Wyman, Dorothy Cantwell, Kelly Connell and Bobo Lewis

l. to r. Richard Seff, Kelly Connell, Pamela Dunlap and Michael Ayr

Dorothy Cantwell, and Kelly Connell

BERNICE: I need to see a man about a dog.

ROGER: Me too.

BERNICE: And maybe some coffee.

ROGER: Oh God, yes.

MARJORIE: Coffee's a good idea.

KEN: Okay, okay, ten minutes.

(BERNICE, ROGER, *and* MARJORIE *exit*)

EDDIE: How's it look so far, Mr. de la Maize?

KEN: It's coming.

O'REILLY: Would anyone be after wantin' anything? I'm goin' to the kitchen for a spot of hot chocolate. *(Which he pronounces "chickelet")*

NIKKI: I'd love some.

KEN: See if she has tea. No, never mind, I'll come myself.

(O'REILLY *exits*. EDDIE *steps in front of* KEN*'s exit*)

EDDIE: Mr. de la Maize, I noticed you skipped over the section where the taxi driver does an imitation of the Japanese ambassador. Well, you don't have to skip it if you don't want to.

KEN: Eddie, I think Roger and Bernice have Bert Lahr in mind for the role of the cab driver.

EDDIE: See, I do a Japanese.

KEN: It needs a name in there, you understand.

EDDIE: I was just thinking it would add flavor.

KEN: I'd be unfair not to tell you that's the direction they're looking.

EDDIE: *(Doing a Japanese—badly)* "You are surplised I speak your ranguage?"

KEN: Your talent is just as special as Lahr's, but I think it is distilled from a different kind of truth. There will probably be other roles which will ring closer to the quality you project. Okay? *(He exits)*

EDDIE: Sure. Thanks a lot, Mr. de la Maize.

(To NIKKI)

What'd he say?

NIKKI: He said, no.

EDDIE: All right, heck, even if I'm just second banana, this could be the break I been waitin' for. Aren't you excited about this?

NIKKI: They usually get stars for the stuff I'm reading, don't they?

EDDIE: Well . . . you never know. *(Watches HER)* You live in New York?

NIKKI: Yes.

EDDIE: Whereabouts?

NIKKI: West Sixty-fourth, between Broadway and Amsterdam.

EDDIE: Yeah? I live on Fiftieth. Across from Madison Square Garden.

NIKKI: I used to live near there. Forty-eighth. The dance belt.

EDDIE: You live alone . . . or . . . ?

NIKKI: I have two roommates.

EDDIE: Got a boyfriend?

NIKKI: Did have. He joined the Navy last year.

EDDIE: Yeah, Navy's not bad. I been thinkin' maybe I should join. 'Fore I get drafted.

NIKKI: Aren't you a bit old to be drafted?

EDDIE: Yeah, right now. But look at the way things are goin'. I figure I better get a name in show business PDQ, so that if I am drafted I can get into the entertainment section of the Army.

NIKKI: You wanna kill 'em with laughs, huh?

EDDIE: They got such units.

NIKKI: A comics' battalion? Yeah, they hit the beach right after the magicians.

EDDIE: It's called Special Services.

NIKKI: Uh-huh, and they pass out Ping-Pong balls.

EDDIE: You know, I'da known you were a dancer even if you never said so.

NIKKI: Yeah?

EDDIE: You talk straight out. Like a guy. Most dames don't talk that way. Dancers do. Course, I'm talkin' show biz, not ballet.

NIKKI: Yeah? What about folk dancers?

EDDIE: I don't know anything about folk dancers except they're mostly long-haired chicks from Bensonhurst.

NIKKI: You date a lot of dancers?

EDDIE: I don't date a lot of anything.

NIKKI: You haven't got a girl?

EDDIE: Nope. See, most dames they don't wanna get serious with a comic.

NIKKI: *(Laughs)* Can you?

EDDIE: If you catch him before coffee. Yeah, but that's okay—that's the way it's laid out.

NIKKI: What's laid out?

EDDIE: The hero gets the girl, the comic gets the laughs.

NIKKI: In the movies.

EDDIE: And in real life . . . pretty much the same.

NIKKI: I wouldn't know. I haven't met any heroes.

EDDIE: Met any comics?

NIKKI: Just one.

(Pause)

I want to look over that second-act ballad.

(NIKKI *sits on the piano bench, looks at the lead sheets.* EDDIE *looks at her.)*

EDDIE: You believe in chemistry?

NIKKI: Chemistry?

EDDIE: You know, you look at someone and something happens.

NIKKI: I don't know.

EDDIE: It's happening here.

(NIKKI *looks at him*)

O'Reilly and the maid. I think we're seeing the start of a hot affair. They really got eyes for each other.

NIKKI: Yeah.

(*Beat . . . then quietly*)

Maybe they sense something in common.

EDDIE: Some people believe in it . . . chemistry. Never happen to you?

NIKKI: Nope.

EDDIE: How about your boyfriend?

NIKKI: We grew up together. He was just . . . always there.

EDDIE: Till now.

NIKKI: Yeah.

EDDIE: Actually it never happened to me either . . . chemistry.

NIKKI: Probably just in the movies.

EDDIE: No. It happened to my father.

NIKKI: Did?

EDDIE: From a bus window. He was on the corner. She was on the bus. They saw each other—Wham! He chased that bus for five blocks.

NIKKI: It was your mother?

EDDIE: No. Some girl. Never saw her again. He used to tell me, "Eddie, when it happens, you'll know. It's chemical. Just hope it ain't the number seventeen to Ozone Park. That's an express."

(NIKKI *laughs and turns back to her music*)

Yeah, it can happen. You just gotta be lookin' for it is all.

(He stares dreamily at her)

(KELLY *enters rolling a tea cart with a full coffee service, cups, etc. He is followed on by* KEN, ROGER, O'REILLY, BERNICE, *and* MARJORIE)

KELLY: So how you all doin'?

KEN: Shall we get back to work?

KELLY: *(Rolls cart to down right)* Miss von Grossenknueten wanted me to lay out some fresh coffee in here for you.

KEN: We just had coffee!

KELLY: So's you won't have to come into the kitchen.

ROGER: She probably just wants us out of the way while she learns to light the oven.

KELLY: So you folks are in the show business, huh?

ROGER: Yes. Do you ever attend the theater, Mr. . . . aah . . .

KELLY: Kelly. No, not too much. I had a cousin in the *Hot Mikado* at the World's Fair.

(ELSA *enters*)

ELSA: Dinner, such as it is, will be around seven. To tide you over, I'll have Helsa bring in some Liederkranz.

KEN: We're fine, Elsa. Please don't worry about us.

(They are all busy around the piano, and they don't notice KELLY *signal to* ELSA *to begin.* ELSA *is not too fast on the uptake)*

ELSA: Now?

(She goes behind the desk, speaks loudly to get their attention)

Oh, and one other thing.

(She looks at KELLY, *who is downstage far right and behind everyone else. He urges her to continue)*

Yesterday, when we were cleaning out the guest rooms in anticipation of your arrivals, guess what we found?

(Pause. She takes the makeup case out of the drawer and sets it on the desk)

Bebe McAllister's makeup kit. It had somehow been packed with the showgirl costumes when the show closed, and sent to Princeton University.

MARJORIE: Showgirl costumes? I thought Princeton was a men's school.

ROGER: Only in the daytime, obviously.

KEN: It's for that show they do. It has a kick line.

ELSA: Last week someone there found the case and, recognizing the name as one of the murder victims, mailed it to the police.

*(*KELLY *signals frantically, "Not to the police, to you.")*

. . . ahhh . . . who thereupon mailed it to me. I put it in the closet and forgot about it. Till yesterday. And with all of us reunited I became curious. I opened it. And what do you think I found?

BERNICE: I don't want to hear this. It's going to be someone's finger or something.

ELSA: A small notebook.

(She looks at KELLY. He smiles and signifies approval by giving her a sign made with thumb and forefinger. She misunderstands.)

A round notebook.

ROGER: A round notebook?

ELSA: Ahh . . . well, a notebook which was . . . full of . . .

(As KELLY is pantomiming writing notes)

. . . notes . . . and . . .

(KELLY dials a phone)

. . . little tiny spirals.

KEN: What?

ELSA: Doodles? . . . Ah, no . . . phone . . . PHONE NUMBERS.

(As KELLY has mimed a phone call. Now he points to his eye and to book)

. . . and . . . something is in my eye . . . no . . . got my eye . . . CAUGHT MY EYE! The last appointment.

(KELLY draws a finger across his throat)

The night she was murdered.

MARJORIE: An appointment with whom?

ELSA: *(As* KELLY *shrugs)* Don't know.

(KELLY *holds up a finger)*

But . . .

(KELLY *points to his watch)*

They were wearing a watch.

(KELLY *is signaling "no")*

No . . . time . . . ahh, the book gives time and place.

KEN: That night? Probably just an appointment to go over a key change or something.

ROGER: Couldn't be. The night poor Bebe was murdered we were dark. No one was at the theater.

KEN: What are you so excited about, Roger?

ROGER: No one was there!

ELSA: (KELLY *is signaling "no")* No, they weren't.

MARJORIE: Weren't what?

ELSA: (KELLY *is mouthing "Not at the theater")* Singing.

BERNICE: What? Who wasn't singing?

ELSA: (KELLY, *still trying to communicate "theater," pulls an imaginary curtain rope to indicate the curtain going up)* They weren't singing . . . in an elevator.

(By now she is near tears in frustration)

No, no—excuse me, I need some coffee.

(She crosses down left to whisper to KELLY)

KEN: Well, the stage manager was at the theater. I remember because the set designer and I stopped by before going to dinner at Toffanetti's.

MARJORIE: Couldn't have been, Ken. The stage manager was with me at the Blue Ribbon.

KEN: No, Marjorie, I remember distinctly because it was the first dark night and—

MARJORIE: I certainly ought to know where my own damn stage manager was, Ken.

KEN: Calm down, Marjorie. Why are you so upset?

ROGER: An alibi, obviously.

ELSA: *(Who has been coached by KELLY)* No, the note doesn't say the theater; it says the hotel. The night she was murdered she had an appointment at the hotel.

MARJORIE: With whom? No one was there.

ROGER: We only used a suite there as a staff room.

KEN: Why don't we take a look at the book?

ELSA: I think it much better if I turn it over to the police *(She points to KELLY, realizes she has goofed, and tries to cover up)* . . . in the morning.

EDDIE: Excuse me, Miss von Grossen . . . aah . . .

NIKKI: . . . knueten.

ELSA: Yes?

EDDIE: Well, maybe you should put that book in a safe place and as far from you as possible. 'Cause if it connects the killer to the murders, he would kill to get it.

ELSA: But he doesn't know I have it, does he?

EDDIE: Well, he does now.

ELSA: Really, Mr. McCuen! For that to be true the killer would have to be in this room.

(All look at one another for a beat)

KEN: Funny, until today I never considered the possibility of its being one of us.

ROGER: I've considered it—constantly.

MARJORIE: Oh, let's not be ridiculous. Of course it isn't one of us. We're show people.

(Quickly) So . . . on with act the second. As Shakespeare might have said.

BERNICE: He might have, but I doubt if he ever did.

ELSA: Do you mind if I watch a bit, Ken? You know how I adore the rehearsal process.

MARJORIE: It will spoil the audition for you, Elsa.

ELSA: I shan't stay long. Just a soupçon.

MARJORIE: No, really, I—

KEN: Oh for God's sake, Marjorie, let her stay! I need to get started.

MARJORIE: *(Indicating wing chair down left)* Sit here, Elsa.

(ELSA *sits)*

KEN: Act Two begins with—

(HELSA *enters with a pot)*

We already have coffee!

HELSA: Fräulein von Grossenknueten mentioned that Herr O'Reilly preferred shokolade.

KEN: All right, all right.

(To BERNICE*)* Bernice, second act, please.

(HELSA *puts the chocolate on tea cart and exits.* O'REILLY *watches, frowning)*

BERNICE: Okay. *White House Merry-Go-Round,* Act Two. It opens in the Senate Chambers. On stage are Biff and Trudy. There are also some pageboys.

MARJORIE: Sounds divoon . . . simply divoon.

(During this, O'REILLY *crosses to the chocolate, pours some, and smells it. No one notices except* KELLY, *who has moved so as to be behind* O'REILLY *to observe him)*

O'REILLY: Excuse me. *(He puts down the chocolate without drinking it)*

KEN: What is it now?

O'REILLY: Sure'n I fear the hot chickelet has gone and given me a terrible headache. I notice I am not needed in this number so if you don't mind, I will step out for some aspirin.

ELSA: (KELLY *signals her to go with* O'REILLY) Oh, you poor, dear boy. There's some in the kitchen. I'll get it for you.

O'REILLY: *(As he and* ELSA *exit)* Thank you.

KEN: Come right back!

BERNICE: That's the format. Here's how it goes. Trudy is opening mail from Biff's constituents, all of whom have advice on how to run the country. This leads to the opener, "Everyone Can Do It Better."

KEN: Okay, so following Bernice's intro, we do the number. Roger . . . ?

(ROGER *is on piano bench,* NIKKI *and* EDDIE *are in the crook of the piano,* KEN *is sitting in center chair,* BERNICE *is to his right,* KELLY *is down right, and* MARJORIE *has sat down in wing chair down left.* ROGER *plays an arpeggio, and suddenly the lights go black. We hear dialogue in the dark.)*

KEN: What happened?

KELLY: Try the light switch.

ROGER: Where is it?

(We hear the sound of someone bumping into something)

EDDIE: Ouch!

KELLY: Everyone just stand still. It may be a power failure. I'm going to the basement.

KEN: Are there any candles?

(We hear a small, stifled scream)

EDDIE: What was that?

ROGER: An owl.

EDDIE: In the library?

BERNICE: This is making me very nervous.

ROGER: Calm down, Bernice.

EDDIE: Hey, I'm not Bernice. Stop rubbing my neck.

ROGER: Sorry.

NIKKI: Let's all remain calm. It's probably the snowstorm. I'm sure Miss von Grossenknueten will be here soon with candles.

BERNICE: Listen, are we all here? Are we? Didn't I hear the tiniest scream a moment ago?

ROGER: Yes, I bumped into the chair.

KEN: We're all here, Bernice.

BERNICE: That's Roger and Ken. This is me. The performers?

EDDIE: I'm here.

NIKKI: And me.

BERNICE: And Marjorie?

(The lights come on. MARJORIE is there. She still sits in her chair, but now about two feet of sword stick out the back of it. She is obviously pinned to the chair in death. But no one notices. Up center, above the door, there is only one sword hanging, instead of two. ELSA enters.)

ELSA: Lights are back. Everyone all right? I think it's because I plugged in the toaster.

KEN: We're fine, Elsa. We're moving as quickly as we can.

ELSA: No hurry. I haven't even started the white sauce. *(She exits)*

KEN and ROGER: White sauce?

ROGER: On sauerbraten?

KEN: C'mon, back to work, kids.

ROGER: From the top.

(ROGER, EDDIE, *and* NIKKI *do the song* "Everyone Can Do It Better")

ALL: Ev'ryone can do it better

EDDIE: from the East Coast to the West

NIKKI: they all know what's really best

ALL: for the U.S.A./Anyone can write a letter

NIKKI: 'bout the way that he or she/wants to run this counter-ee

ALL: if they have their way./they all know just what to do/about internal revenue/and the kinda bones . . ./

ROGER: that Fala oughta chew./

ALL: Yeah, they all can do it better/and after all of this advice,/ darlin' it feels very nice/to be here with you./

KEN: Take it home!

ALL: 'Cause when it comes to us/no one does it better/than just we two-oo-oo!/

(During song, BERNICE has walked over to MARJORIE for a reaction, and getting none, goes back to center, very upset. At

end of song all look to MARJORIE *for a response again. Naturally there is none.)*

EDDIE: *(To* NIKKI*)* I don't think she liked it.

NIKKI: She's smiling, see? She's just not being vocal.

BERNICE: *(To* MARJORIE*)* Well, following that number, which will be catchier and funnier . . . or maybe cut, if you hate it that much!

ROGER: Bernice, let's go on.

BERNICE: No, I mean that's the second-act opener. And if she hates it . . .

KEN: All right . . . Marjorie, do you hate it or is Bernice going through a typical attack of paranoia?

(They wait)

ROGER: Marjorie, honey . . . we're friends here. I mean if you've got something to say, let's say it now and not sit there acting like a typical producer.

(Suddenly the revolving bookcase moves and KELLY *steps out, gun in hand)*

KELLY: Someone pulled the main breaker. Has anyone—

*(*KELLY *notices* MARJORIE, *crosses to her and pulls out sword. She falls to the floor.* NIKKI *rushes to her.)*

NIKKI: *(Feeling pulse)* She's dead!

ROGER: Dead! My God!

EDDIE: *(Goes to* BERNICE*)* Well, that should make you feel better. At least it wasn't the song.

KELLY: Has anyone come into the room from the passageway, and out the door?

BERNICE: I was by the door. They'd have had to pass through me to—Oh my God, a ghost!

KELLY: I'll check the hall. *(He exits)*

EDDIE: How about here? *(He goes to French doors)*

ROGER: Call the police!

BERNICE: Police! Police! Police!

ROGER: On the phone, Bernice!

EDDIE: Frozen shut.   KEN: The phone is dead, remember.

EDDIE: The closet!

KEN: The closet!

ROGER: The closet!

BERNICE: The phone is in the closet?

(BERNICE opens the closet door. A dead HELSA, clad in panties and bra, falls forward and right into BERNICE's arms.)

Roger, would you hold this for a moment please.

(ROGER grabs HELSA. BERNICE walks downstage, getting lower and lower, and faints dead away.)

EDDIE: *(Looks at the three bodies lying on stage, turns to KEN)* Does this mean the show's canceled?

Act Two

ACT TWO

(At rise . . . NIKKI *is stage left.* BERNICE *is below the piano with an ice pack on her head.* ROGER *is coming down center shaking a martini shaker. The wind howls. The clock is striking five.)*

ROGER: I should have listened to my numerologist. She said stay out of Westchester County. It adds up to death and decay.

BERNICE: Poor Marjorie. She had so many things to live for. *(Beat)* Though at the moment I can't think of a single one.

ROGER: I fear Elsa has brought the Stage Door Slasher to Chappaqua.

BERNICE: You think? It couldn't just be someone who wanted Marjorie dead? The Shuberts, maybe?

NIKKI: What about Helsa?

(EDDIE, KEN, *and* KELLY *enter)*

KEN: We put them in a snowdrift. It's the best we could do under the circumstances. It's a blizzard out there. You can't see a foot in front of you.

EDDIE: Or the rest of the body, for that matter.

KELLY: This coffee hot? Jeez, it's brutal out there.

EDDIE: This hot chocolate?

KELLY: Don't touch that!

EDDIE: What?

KELLY: I'm no expert, but that stuff smells to me like it was poisoned. I noticed just 'fore the lights went out that O'Reilly sniffed it and wouldn't—Hey, where the hell is he, anyway?

NIKKI: That's the sixty-four-dollar question.

BERNICE: *(Going to tea cart)* Elsa probably used too much salt.

ROGER: You put salt in hot chocolate?

BERNICE: Sure. Should be only a tad, of course, but it really gives it some snap.

ROGER: I've never thought of that. I've tried a dab of nutmeg, but I didn't find that to be—

EDDIE: Nutmeg? In hot chocolate?

KELLY: Could we leave the recipe exchange till tomorrow? We got a killer loose here!

(ELSA *enters with roll of dusty blueprints)*

ELSA: I've found the blueprints!

KEN: What blueprints?

ELSA: Of the estate. Since whoever cut off the power escaped through the tunnels, I thought if we examined these we might find details of those passages. Then we could foray into the walls to look for clues. I'll put together a picnic lunch in case we get lost.

KELLY: *(Examining blueprints)* These just show the house. They don't show the passageways.

ELSA: Of course not. They're secret.

KELLY: Right now, I want everybody where I can see 'em.

ELSA: And I want to look for clues!

KELLY: I'm in charge of this investigation and I say you are staying here!

KEN: Investigation? What investigation?

KELLY: Murder investigation. I'm a cop.

ELSA: Why are you telling them?

KELLY: This has gone too far for adventures, Miss von Grossenknueten.

(To others)

I'm Sergeant Michael Kelly of the New York City Police Department, here on the case of the Stage Door Slasher.

EDDIE: So it's not an audition?

KEN: Only for a killer, it seems.

EDDIE: Just my luck.

ROGER: I told you, I told you, I told you. But did you listen? No, I'm just a silly songwriter. I did go to the Boston Conservatory, you know.

ELSA: I think this exposure unwise, Sergeant.

KELLY: The killer is working too damn fast. He didn't go for you and the notebook. He went for someone who obviously could expose him somehow. And not just once. We've had two murders. Maybe three. Maybe four, if we count O'Reilly.

ROGER: Who was maybe three?

KELLY: There are bloodstains by the French doors.

KEN: But nobody else is missing.

KELLY: Nobody we *know* about.

BERNICE: You mean there could be someone missing who wasn't here in the first place?

ROGER: But if you're the police, what was all that business about notifying them in regard to Bebe's book?

KELLY: A setup.

ELSA: I was to be the bait, Roger. When the killer came for me—and the notebook—the sergeant would capture him. Clever, yes?

ROGER: It was, until you told us all about it.

KELLY: Obviously some other people were more dangerous to the killer than this book.

NIKKI: Perhaps it's a combination of that book and those other people that worried the killer. With them out of the way, the book is useless.

KELLY: That's exactly the way I got it pegged, miss.

ELSA: I still maintain we should examine these blueprints. The chase is half the fun.

ROGER: Let me get this straight. All that nonsense about Bebe's notebook was just made up in order to . . .

KELLY: No, the book is the real McCoy. Sent to the department from Princeton last week. And it contains information that made us reopen the case.

KEN: What sort of information?

KELLY: Look at the last entry.

(He gives book to KEN. ROGER *rushes to look also)*

KEN: Picadilly, 1020.

BERNICE: My God!

ELSA: What is it, Bernice?

BERNICE: I just got the new second-act opener.

(She rushes to the desk)

Give me a pen!

(She moves the penholder and the bookcase revolves)

That is so annoying!

(She moves it again and the bookcase closes)

ROGER: Well, the Picadilly was our hotel in New York. What's 1020?

KELLY: Your room.

ROGER: My room!

KELLY: And the rest of the artistic staff. It's Bebe McAllister's last appointment. The night of the murder.

KEN: Oh yes, that was all that stuff that Elsa was talking about earlier. Well, obviously it didn't worry the killer too much.

ROGER: Why should it? The staff suite. My God! I mean the key was left at the desk. Everyone—designers, stage manager—everyone had access to those rooms. You reopened the investigation based on that one appointment?

KELLY: We were hopin' it might lead to something.

ROGER: Well, obviously it didn't.

KELLY: Obviously it did. There are two people dead.

EDDIE: Wait a second. The thing I can't figure is why Bebe was in the hotel at all. Show's off the road, everyone's staying at home. It's a day off when the murder happens. Now, what's a chorus girl do on her day off?

(All look at NIKKI*)*

NIKKI: Huh? Oh . . . well . . .

EDDIE: Sleeps.

NIKKI: Well, she certainly wouldn't go near where a murderer was loose.

KEN: I would think Bebe would want to spend that time with friends—wouldn't you, Elsa?

ELSA: Poor Bebe had many dear friends, Ken.

KEN: Too many?

ROGER: There's a list following the appointment . . . in parentheses. Twenty-two, toe shoes, leo. Then a series of numbers —2-8-8-1-2-9 . . . Leo could be something astrological.

KEN: Isn't twenty-two a type of gun?

KELLY: Caliber, yeah. We wondered about that. But there was no gun involved.

NIKKI: Twenty-two. Tu-tu.

EDDIE: What?

NIKKI: *(Crossing to look at notebook)* Tutu, toe shoes, leo, leotard. Sounds like the appointment was for a ballet class. Though why she'd wear a tutu is beyond me.

KELLY: What's it look like?

NIKKI: A tutu? It's a little skirt. Very stiff. Sticks out in front like—

(KEN, ROGER, *and* EDDIE *all mime "tutu" at the same time as* NIKKI)

KELLY: She had it on.

KEN: What?

KELLY: We didn't release that to the press. She had it on. So did the other two.

ROGER: Murdered in a tutu?

NIKKI: How were they wearing their hair?

KELLY: Hair?

NIKKI: Yeah. Was that the same too?

KELLY: Now that you mention it, it was. Tight. Pulled back like a schoolteacher.

NIKKI: Ballet dancers. The Slasher was killing ballet dancers.

EDDIE: Why?

ROGER: He probably sat through *Les Sylphides* one time too many.

NIKKI: What I mean is, they were dressed like ballet dancers. As if it was some kind of audition or act.

BERNICE: Anyone want to hear the new lyric? I think I've caught the real flavor of Washington with it. It's called "Ways, Means, and Mischief."

(She crosses to the piano bench)

I'll take it from the chorus.

(HELSA *appears in the hall with a feather duster. Only* BERNICE *sees her at first, and with a loud bang on the piano keys, collapses on the floor in a faint*)

ELSA: Poor Bernice, she works herself much too hard.

NIKKI: Helsa!

ROGER: You're dead!

ELSA: Helsa, my God!

HELSA: I beg your pardon?

EDDIE: Maybe the cold revived her.

KELLY: Don't anybody move! *(He runs out)*

HELSA: *Was ist los?*

KEN: Helsa, we saw you half-naked and dead fall from the closet into Bernice's arms.

ROGER: *(Remembers that* BERNICE *is still out cold)* Oh, Bernice!

HELSA: Perhaps it was someone else. I was in the basement gathering potatoes for the vichyssoise.

KELLY: *(Running back in)* She's still out there—dead.

HELSA: Who is dead?

KEN: Helsa, have you a twin?

HELSA: *Ja,* two. I am of triplets. Sisters. But they are in Germany.

ELSA: Helsa, someone who looks very like you was . . . murdered here this afternoon.

HELSA: I will look.

KELLY: Come, this way.

HELSA: *(Starts to exit, stops)* My mutter und vater worked in Berlin as laborers in the government printing plant. In 1923 they died when a carton which contained marks the equivalent of five American dollars fell on them und they were crushed. My sisters und I were raised by relatives. We saw each other only on Weihnachtsabend, when we met to decorate the Weihnachtsbaum, und give out Weihnachtsgeschenke.

EDDIE: Gesundheit!

HELSA: My point is, I did not know my sisters! *(She exits, followed by KELLY)*

EDDIE: That woman has absolutely no sense of humor.

KEN: *(To ELSA)* Did Helsa accompany you out of town during *Manhattan Holiday?*

ELSA: No, Helsa was here at the house.

NIKKI: My gosh, identical triplets, a homicidal maniac, secret passages . . .

EDDIE: Yeah, it's beginning to look like one of those Hollywood mysteries you direct, Mr. de la Maize.

ROGER: I didn't know you had directed a mystery, Ken.

KEN: One. *Murder at the Biltmore,* with William Powell, Myrna Loy, Sidney Blackmer, Ralph Bellamy, Nat Pendleton, Louise Albritton, and Elisha Cook, Jr.

NIKKI: Has that *been* released?

KEN: No. Have you seen it?

NIKKI: I think so.

(HELSA enters to center. All stare, waiting for a reply)

HELSA: I don't think she looks a thing like me.

(She crosses down right and starts wheeling the tea cart out the door)

ELSA: But Helsa . . .

KELLY: *(Entering)* She's the spit 'n' image.

NIKKI: Was either of your sisters a ballet dancer, by any chance?

HELSA: Dancers! *Gott in Himmel,* no. Hilda lives in Stralsund working in a boatyard making sails. Helga lives in Stuttgart where she waits table in a beer garten. Now, if you will excuse me, I must get back to the dinner.

KELLY: You're sayin' that's not your sister out there?

HELSA: Anything is possible, but I believe my sisters to be in Germany.

KELLY: That woman out there is an exact likeness.

HELSA: My Grossvater was a merchant seaman out of Bremen. Perhaps he put ashore in Brooklyn. It is only a train ride to here . . . *nicht wahr?*

(Starts to go . . . stops)

Mr. O'Reilly is dead also?

KELLY: We don't know.

(HELSA *runs out, pushing the cart ahead of her*)

EDDIE: *(To* NIKKI) I told you she had eyes for him. Two murders and all she's concerned for is O'Reilly.

ELSA: Obviously Helsa is lying. Though I can't imagine why.

EDDIE: She's covering for him.

KELLY: I thought espionage was in your blood.

ELSA: It is. It's just a little sluggish at the moment.

NIKKI: Maybe her sister was on her way here and was killed before Helsa knew she arrived.

KEN: So why wouldn't she identify her?

ROGER: Perhaps Helsa's sister is the Slasher.

ELSA: If her sister is the Slasher, then who slashed her?

ROGER: It's all too confusing.

EDDIE: Naw. It's simple. Look, you got a sister who's a servant in Chappaqua, a sister selling sausage and sauerkraut in Stuttgart, and a sister sewing sails somewhere.

NIKKI: Stralsund.

EDDIE: Soo . . . either Helga from Stuttgart or Hilda from Stralsund, while seeking her sister in a snowstorm in a swanky, secluded section of Chappaqua, is stabbed by the Slasher who thinks Hilda or Helga is Helsa. Now . . . ask yourself why.

ROGER: Ask myself why? I don't even know what you said!

KEN: Ask myself why what?

EDDIE: Not why what, why who?

KEN: Why who what?

KELLY: No, not why who what, why why what?

KEN: Why why who what why?

ROGER: What?

KELLY: Because before you ask who, you have to ask why.

ELSA: And how.

ROGER: How what?

ELSA: I was just agreeing. And how.

NIKKI: Maybe it depends on when.

KEN and EDDIE: WHEN WHAT?

BERNICE: Please! If you're going to do that again, I need another drink. *(She crosses to bar)*

EDDIE: Let me see that book.

KEN: Could Helsa be the Stage Door Slasher? Well, it's what we're all thinking, right?

ELSA: Oh, that's what we're all thinking. But why would Helsa murder three women?

ROGER: Jealousy.

ELSA: Of whom?

ROGER: Of your friends, of course. You said you had many.

ELSA: I said Bebe had many.

KEN: Really, Roger, if you are going to take the thoughts of others and twist them, I prefer you stick to Jerome Kern; you do that so much better.

ROGER: I do not steal from Jerome Kern!

BERNICE: He certainly does not!

ROGER: Thank you, Bernice.

BERNICE: It's Sigmund Romberg.

ROGER: Oh fine, fine, let's all be viciously funny about my talent. It strikes me as an exceptionally transparent attempt to get us off the subject—which is, Which one of us might have had a motive?

KEN: Fine. Shall we begin with the well-known fact that you hate dancers?

ROGER: Not true. I only hate them when they sing.

KEN: You did demand that those three girls be removed from the numbers.

ROGER: But not with a knife, Ken.

KEN: My point is, we can come up with a motive for any of us. Even me. They were all pregnant, or something. But I don't think the killer is in this room.

NIKKI: What about O'Reilly? We haven't seen him since the blackout.

KELLY: He may be dead.

NIKKI: Or in those tunnels.

ELSA: Well, we won't know if we don't look. I am going to serve dinner. And then I suggest an armed foray into those walls.

(Stops at door)

There is another possibility. Perhaps Helsa is her sister.

KELLY: What?

ELSA: Just something that happened earlier. When I attempted to kiss her good morning. Something . . . different. *(She exits)*

EDDIE: She kisses her maid good morning?

KELLY: Okay, now I want to get to solving this thing. So I want to reconstruct the moment before the crime. I want all of you to show me where you were standing when the lights went out.

ROGER: You've got to be kidding!

EDDIE: No, this can work. Ellery Queen does it all the time.

KEN: All right, all right, let's try it. I was here. Bernice, where were you?

ROGER: She was over there.   BERNICE: I was behind the chair.

NIKKI and EDDIE: We were here. *(All go to their positions)*

KEN: *(Indicating wing chair)* And poor Marjorie was over there.

KELLY: *(Looking at them one by one)* Hm . . . hm . . . hm . . .

(Ends up behind wing chair, looks at them again)

This doesn't tell me a goddamn thing!

KEN: Well, I for one do not think we should leave Elsa alone in the kitchen with Helsa. *(He exits)*

BERNICE: Wait a second, Ken. I want to read you the new lyric.

ROGER: Personally, I thought what we had originally was fine.

BERNICE: Marjorie hated it.

ROGER: Marjorie was dead, Bernice. I don't think you should allow a dead woman's opinion to influence you.

(ROGER *and* BERNICE *exit*)

EDDIE: I can't believe one of them could be the Slasher.

KELLY: Naw, I doubt they are. I got me a whole other theory.

EDDIE: *(To* NIKKI*)* You comin' to the kitchen?

NIKKI: *(Reading Bebe's notebook)* In a sec.

EDDIE: You find something interesting?

NIKKI: It's addresses . . . appointments . . . and a kind of log. She refers to things she's done that day. See, "LN" . . . small "w" . . . slash "K".

KELLY: Lunch with Kathy. 'Nother dancer in the show. We already checked all those notes out. The ones we could make sense of anyway.

NIKKI: I think it's a code.

EDDIE: Code? Why would she keep a code?

NIKKI: Every so often there's nothing but a list of numbers.

KELLY: Phone numbers.

NIKKI: But there's not always an exchange. Here's Endicott . . . Murray Hill . . . but then rows of numbers. It's a code.

EDDIE: Bank accounts, maybe. Secret bank accounts!

NIKKI: Yeah, maybe.

KELLY: I got a theory. And it's based on plain old-fashioned police work.

EDDIE: Hey, maybe serial numbers.

KELLY: Observation. Observation, that's the key. And if I'm right, then someone is in very great danger. And I think I know who that someone . . .

(The bookcase behind him, up right, slides open enough for an arm to come out and, choking KELLY *around the throat, pull him back into the opening. The wall slides shut.* EDDIE *and* NIKKI, *bent over the notebook, see nothing of this.)*

NIKKI: Maybe the numbers are letter substitutes.

EDDIE: Where'd you learn about that?

NIKKI: When you were a kid didn't you ever send away to Orphan Annie or Jack Armstrong for a secret decoder?

EDDIE: Don Winslow of the Navy. I got a ring.

NIKKI: Well, I'll use the Orphan Annie system. Let's try to break it.

EDDIE: What we need is paper.

(He pulls open a desk drawer. This causes a section of the bookcase down left to slide open revealing another passage.)

Holy mackerel! I opened the desk drawer and . . . Hey, Sarge—

(Looks for KELLY*)*

Where'd the cop go?

NIKKI: My gosh, another tunnel!

EDDIE: This joint has more surprises than Sal Hepatica.

NIKKI: There are steps leading down.

EDDIE: Are you nuts? Don't go in there!

NIKKI: I want to see what's down here.

(She enters tunnel)

EDDIE: If you run into the Slasher, don't plié!

NIKKI: *(Off stage)* It looks like a wine cellar.

EDDIE: Great, now come back up. I can't believe you're doing
this when there's a killer loose.

(The upstage left bookcase revolves and a FIGURE *. . . dressed
in a black trench coat, black slouch hat, and a black hood over
its face with eye holes cut out . . . steps onstage.* EDDIE, *who is
looking into tunnel down left does not see or hear* FIGURE.)

I mean, there's someone, maybe a raving maniac, in this house,
with a knife or a saber and you're walking around down there
in the dark instead of staying up here in the light where it's
safe.

*(*FIGURE *is at desk reaching for notebook when* EDDIE *turns and
sees it.)*

Oh my God! Hi! Can I help you? All the dancers are out right
now, but if you'd care to leave a message . . .

(The FIGURE *pulls out an enormous straight razor)*

No thanks, I shaved earlier. Besides, I have a regular barber. Frank, at the Astor, you know him?

(FIGURE *lunges at him*)

Oh I get it—you think I'm a dancer. *(Laughs)* That agent of mine. He'll tell anybody anything to get me work. No, I'm a comic.

(FIGURE *lunges again.* EDDIE *scurries under piano,* FIGURE *hops up on piano bench.* EDDIE *looks around and doesn't see it. As* EDDIE *starts crawling to center on all fours,* FIGURE *steps behind him with razor.* EDDIE *thinks* FIGURE *is gone, so he stands up and brushes himself off, and as he brushes his knees he also brushes the knee of the* FIGURE, *who has placed foot between* EDDIE's. EDDIE *ducks just as* FIGURE *slashes with razor, and* EDDIE *starts out the door followed by* FIGURE. *They are both stopped by* NIKKI's *voice from the tunnel.)*

NIKKI: *(Off stage)* There are more passages down here.

(FIGURE *spins and, holding razor high, rushes toward tunnel*)

EDDIE: In addition to being a comic, I'm also a ventriloquist! Throw my voice anywhere—wine cellars . . .

NIKKI: *(Off stage)* Eddie!

EDDIE: *(Falsetto)* Eddie!

(FIGURE *steps toward tunnel.* EDDIE *dashes to desk and slams drawer shut. Wall closes in* FIGURE's *face.* FIGURE *spins toward* EDDIE. EDDIE *grabs notebook.)*

EDDIE: Lookin' for this?

(FIGURE *starts for* EDDIE. EDDIE *runs out center door.* FIGURE *is heading for door when closet opens and out steps* HELSA. FIGURE *and* HELSA *face each other for a moment.* HELSA *is holding up meat cleaver,* FIGURE *is holding up razor. Down left, book-*

case begins to move. HELSA *and* FIGURE *see this.* HELSA *darts back into closet.* FIGURE *disappears into revolving bookcase. Down left wall slides open and* NIKKI *reenters.)*

NIKKI: Eddie, why'd you shut—Eddie?

EDDIE: *(Running back in)* All-ee, all-ee in free! Hey, where'd he go? Where'd he go? I'll clip him, so help me, I'll mow him down.

NIKKI: Eddie, did you shut me in there as some kind of joke?

EDDIE: How'd you get out of there?

NIKKI: There's a lever next to the door.

EDDIE: The Slasher was here.

NIKKI: The Slasher was here?

EDDIE: While you were down there. Right here, in a long rain-coat with a bag over his head.

NIKKI: What'd he look like?

EDDIE: Like somebody in a long raincoat with a bag over his head.

NIKKI: No, I mean—tall, short?

EDDIE: Who knows? Both, maybe. I was busy lookin' at the razor.

NIKKI: Let's go tell the others.

EDDIE: No, it could be one of them. *(Holds up notebook)* He was after this, but I grabbed it and ran.

NIKKI: You did? Gee, Eddie, you're kinda brave.

EDDIE: Naw, just fast. See, when you play some of the joints I play . . . *(He is looking around for a safe place to hide the notebook.)*

NIKKI: Which one of them do you think it is?

EDDIE: Well, I got a theory, based on observation.

(He has opened and closed the desk drawer to put the notebook away. But that opened the down left wall, allowing O'REILLY *to come in, with a gun, trapping him in the room as the wall closes.)*

NIKKI: O'Reilly!

EDDIE: We thought you were dead!

O'REILLY: *(Quickly hides gun, pulls out a handkerchief and holds it to his forehead.)* Sure and so did somebody else. I was hit on me head and left to die. *(He staggers to center chair)*

NIKKI: When was this?

O'REILLY: When I was goin' for the aspirin.

EDDIE: Hope you got a chance to take a couple.

O'REILLY: When I come to, I found myself in a tunnel and I've had the devil's own time tryin' to get out.

NIKKI: There have been two murders here!

EDDIE: And what's more, it isn't even an audition. It's a setup to catch the Slasher.

O'REILLY: Murders? Who?

EDDIE: Miss Baverstock, and someone who's either Helsa, Hilda, or Helga.

O'REILLY: Was?

NIKKI: Someone who we think is Helsa's twin sister.

EDDIE: Fell right out of that closet.

O'REILLY: Her sister, was it? And Helsa? She is all right?

EDDIE: Yeah, fine, don't worry. *(Winks at* NIKKI) She was concerned about you too.

O'REILLY: Was she, now? Faith, and she's a fine soup of a lass. *(Rises)* I believe I'll have a spot of brandy to ward off the chill.

EDDIE: Sit still, I'll get it. *(Crosses to bar)*

NIKKI: So, how long have you been in this country, Mr. O'Reilly?

O'REILLY: What?

NIKKI: I asked how long you'd been in America. You are Irish-born?

O'REILLY: As Paddy's cow.

NIKKI: And where in Ireland are you from?

O'REILLY: Sure'n are you familiar with Ireland, colleen?

NIKKI: I've never been there, no.

(EDDIE *hands* O'REILLY *drink)*

O'REILLY: Well, there's a spot in County Blarney which the sun, comin' over the MacNamara mountains, hits first; coverin' the River Donegal with a dress of shimmerin' silver so as to please a saint's wife. And wakin' the fine village of . . . McGillicuddy to another of God's days. It's there that I'm from and it's there that I'll ever be.

EDDIE: *(To* NIKKI*)* You oughta know better than to ask an Irishman where he's from. We coulda been here all night.

O'REILLY: *(Sipping drink)* Sure'n it's as warmin' as a bog of peat in August.

NIKKI: Have I seen you in anything on Broadway, Mr. O'Reilly?

O'REILLY: *(With a deadly smile)* Are you writin' a book about me, miss?

ELSA: *(Entering with tiny dinner bell)* Dinner is served. Oh, Mr. O'Reilly, you've returned to us.

EDDIE: Somebody hit him on the head and left him to die.

ELSA: My dear, we've unleashed something horrible in this house tonight. However, the vichyssoise is ready and—where is Sergeant Kelly?

EDDIE: I don't know. Isn't he with you?

ELSA: Perhaps he went to wash up. Come along, everyone else is in the dining room. Let's eat so we can get down to the serious business of the evening.

*(*ELSA *exits.* O'REILLY *puts glass down on piano and follows her out.)*

NIKKI: I don't think he's Irish.

EDDIE: Easy enough to tell. We'll give him some more brandy and see if he starts to fight, sing, or write a poem.

(As they are exiting, O'REILLY *reenters.)*

O'REILLY: Begorrah, I went and forgot me drink.

(He is alone in the room. He closes the door)

Dinner is served, Helsa! *(Laughs)* Helsa? They tell me your sister is dead. Are you in mourning? *(Laughs)* Helsa, come out. I think we should talk.

(He pulls a revolver from his coat and cocks it. He moves the penholder. Bookcase pivots—no one is there. He walks to bookcases, studying them for another panel. He is backing up center when suddenly HELSA bursts out of closet, screaming in fury and brandishing the meat cleaver. He whirls just in time to duck as she plants the cleaver into a book. It stays there. She slams his wrist against the wall, forcing him to drop the gun. She lunges for the letter opener on the desk. He tries to stop her but misses. They meet center, struggling. She twists free and drives the blade upward. It slices through O'REILLY's belt. His trousers fall to his ankles. He grabs HELSA, forcing her back across the desk, and the letter opener falls. They now commence attempting to strangle each other, making loud and fierce sounds of exertion. HELSA, who is bent back across the desk, throws her legs around O'REILLY's back to lock him to her.

At this point EDDIE enters.)

EDDIE: Uh . . . excuse me . . . I didn't mean to . . . they sent me back for the wine and . . . uh . . .

(He shields his eyes as he crosses to the bar down right)

I'm not looking. Just going for wine. Don't let me interrupt.

(Gets to the bar)

Gee . . . they didn't say if they wanted white or red. Well, I'll just take one of each.

(Crosses back to door)

Sorry to have bothered you. I'll tell them to save you something.

(NIKKI enters. He puts a hand over her eyes)

Hey, don't look. *(Whispers)* O'Reilly and the maid.

(At this point HELSA *breaks arm loose and unloads a terrific right on* O'REILLY.*)*

Gee, and they were getting along so well.

NIKKI: I'm going for help. *(She runs out)*

EDDIE: *(Shouts after her)* Hey, ask whether we're having meat or fish!

(HELSA *runs through the revolving bookcase.* O'REILLY *scrambles for the gun and follows her out.* NIKKI, KEN, ELSA, *and* ROGER *run on center)*

NIKKI: Where'd they go?

EDDIE: Into the wall.

NIKKI: He's trying to kill her. We've got to help.

KEN: Help how?

ROGER: Where's that cop?

NIKKI: I'm going into that tunnel.

KEN: Are you crazy? Don't go in there!

EDDIE: It's useless to try to stop her, believe me.

NIKKI: We can't just stand here and do nothing.

BERNICE: *(Enters, carrying a bottle of wine and glass)* Sure we can.

ELSA: We need to trap him from two directions. *(Spreading blueprints on floor)* Look, Nikki, you're going in through here. I'll enter from the billiard room.

ROGER: That's the billiard room?

ELSA: Yes.

ROGER: Interesting you would place it over here next to the parlor.

ELSA: Well, it used to be the music room, you see, but . . .

BERNICE: I would have put it closer to the solarium.

KEN: Can we hold the architectural discussion till later?

NIKKI: He may be killing her! I'm going in.

EDDIE: I'll go with you. Two can die as easy as one.

ELSA: *(Getting flashlight from desk)* Here, take this flashlight so you can see what you are up against.

EDDIE: See it? Who wants to see it?

NIKKI: Play the radio very loud. That way we can always find this room.

EDDIE: If you can find the Red Network of NBC, Phil Spitalny and his all-girl orchestra is on right now.

(EDDIE *and* NIKKI *have gone into revolving passage up left.* ROGER *turns on the radio.)*

ELSA: I warn you, it's a labyrinth in there. Stay close together!

(We hear "Jeanie with the Light Brown Hair")

Please, Roger, anything but that.

(ROGER *spins dial)*

RADIO (VO): . . . buried under snow in this blizzard fast reaching catastrophic proportions. Transportation has halted. Governor Lehman and Mayor La Guardia have declared that a state of emergency . . .

ROGER: My God, all we need now is a power failure!

(The lights go out)

BERNICE: From your mouth to God's ear.

ELSA: There are storm lanterns in the pantry. Come help me get them.

ROGER: Ouch! Dammit, I just bumped into the piano.

BERNICE: That was my head.

ELSA: Are you coming, Roger?

KEN: Are you still sitting on the floor, Bernice?

BERNICE: I'm not moving until the lights come back on. I'm just going to sit here with this bottle of wine and relax.

ELSA: All right, Bernice. We'll be back for you. Come on.

(ELSA, ROGER, *and* KEN *exit. A pause . . . then we hear* BERNICE *singing.)*

BERNICE: "There's mischief in Washington and it's happening every day . . ."

(The closet door starts to creak open. BERNICE *stops singing, listens a moment, then continues)*

"There's mix-ups in Washington and guess who has to pay?"

(Another noise. She calls out pleasantly.)

Who is it?

(HELSA *darts out of the closet holding a candle, wearing a coat, and carrying a small bag. She heads for French doors, sees* BERNICE *and crosses quickly to her.* HELSA *pulls out a butcher knife and places it at* BERNICE's *throat.*)

HELSA: You have not seen me.

BERNICE: *(Terrified)* Not in years.

HELSA: *(Crosses to French doors but cannot get them open) Ach! Das ist eingefroren!*

ROGER: *(Off)* Ken, where are you?

KEN: *(Off)* In the corridor!

(HELSA *moves quickly back to* BERNICE *and puts knife at her throat.*)

HELSA: I am going back into that closet. You will not tell them you saw me.

BERNICE: My lips are sealed.

HELSA: If you tell, I will drag you into the tunnels where no one can find you. Have you ever been stripped, tied to a wall, and whipped?

(Long pause)

Well?

BERNICE: Do I have to answer that?

ELSA: *(Off stage)* Aah, here, here's the library.

HELSA: *(Running back to closet door, turns to* BERNICE*)* Remember . . . one word and you die!

(HELSA dashes into closet, just as ELSA, ROGER, and KEN enter carrying lanterns.)

BERNICE: She's in the closet! She's in the closet!

ELSA: Who?

BERNICE: Helsa! She's in the closet!

ELSA: Really? What is she . . . ?

(She opens closet. HELSA stands poised with the knife raised. ELSA screams.)

KEN: My God!

(ELSA and KEN slam closet door shut and lock it.)

ROGER: Just keep her locked up till help comes.

ELSA: I'm going for that police officer. Stay here in case he comes out of the walls. *(She exits)*

ROGER: Out of the walls? Oh yes, I forgot we're visiting the House of Usher.

BERNICE: *(Getting up)* Out of the walls? Out of the walls? That's it, Roger. The second act opener should be a waltz! Dick Rogers does one every show.

ROGER: Bernice, this is hardly the place and it certainly isn't the time.

BERNICE: Isn't the time, Roger? Isn't the time? I'm creating. Don't tell me it isn't the time. The contractions are beginning and he tells me it isn't the time. I've been stopped from giving birth a lot here tonight, Ken.

(Bookcase down left opens and O'REILLY steps out)

O'REILLY: Has anyone seen the maid?

BERNICE: She's in the closet.

(O'REILLY *starts for closet*)

KEN: She's got a butcher knife.

O'REILLY: I've got a gun.

ROGER: What's an Irish tenor doing with a gun?

O'REILLY: I'm not Irish, I'm Italian. *(Showing* KELLY's *badge)* Lieutenant Tony Garibaldi, N.Y.P.D. Working undercover on da case of da Stage Door Slasher. The maid is the Slasher and she's on her way up the river.

(To closet) Okay, Wenzel, the jig's up, come out with your hands high.

(Pause) You hoid me, Wenzel, you're trapped!

(Pause) Okay, Wenzel, I'm countin' to ten. *Eins, Zwei, Drei* . . .

ROGER: He's counting in German!

KEN: Well, Helsa's German.

O'REILLY: . . . *Vier, Fünf* . . .

ROGER: *Fünf?*

BERNICE: Five.

ROGER: No wonder they're so broke over there.

O'REILLY: . . . *Acht, Neun, Zehn.*

(Pause)

KEN: Actually, she couldn't come out even if she wanted to—the door's locked.

O'REILLY: Well, unlock it!

(KEN *unlocks door and opens it as they stand back.* EDDIE *steps out, blinking)*

EDDIE: Hi! Boy, am I glad to see you. The flashlight went out and we've been wandering around in pitch black. Would have gotten separated but I held her hand and led her through the tunnels. C'mon Nikki, we're back in the house.

(He reaches hand back and pulls out KELLY *who is bound with his tie and gagged with a napkin.)*

Where'd you come from? What happened to Nikki?

KELLY: Umm brr ydss grubbledk.

EDDIE: What?

KELLY: *(More insistent)* Umm brr ydss grubbledk.

EDDIE: Wait a minute, I can't understand a thing you're saying.

(Removes gag)

Now, what did you say?

KELLY: I said, take this goddamn gag outa my mouth!

(EDDIE *unties* KELLY's *hands)*

O'REILLY: Did you just pass the maid in there?

EDDIE: Who knows? It's too dark to see anything.

KEN: Helsa is the Stage Door Slasher.

EDDIE: Helsa? Wait a minute, and she's in there? With Nikki?

O'REILLY: I'll take care of this.

(EDDIE *starts for closet,* KELLY *grabs him*)

KELLY: No, hold it. This is a job for the police.

KEN: But he is the police. Lieutenant Tony Somebody.

ROGER: He's working on the Slasher case.

KELLY: Outa where?

O'REILLY: Headquarters.

KELLY: What division?

O'REILLY: Eerie crimes.

KELLY: Eerie crimes division?

O'REILLY: Yeah, it's a new thing the Commissioner just . . .

KELLY: You gotta badge?

ROGER: Of course he has a badge. He just showed it to us.

KELLY: C'mon pal, let's see some I.D.

O'REILLY: Sure.

(Takes a step back, cocking and leveling gun)

Hands up! Everyone, over there.

(Motions to right wall. All the men run to right, with hands up. O'REILLY *has crossed to desk to pick up lantern, sees* BERNICE *sitting there, and gestures "nah."*)

KELLY: It's my badge, right? You're the son of a bitch conked me on the head, right?

O'REILLY: I needed the I.D. Almost worked. Till bumblenuts here spoiled everything.

EDDIE: Hey, just a minute . . .

(ELSA *enters from door with lantern.*)

ELSA: I can't find that police officer anywhere.

KEN: Careful, Elsa!

(They are waving at her to go back, she mistakes it for a greeting.)

ELSA: Oh, hello everyone.

O'REILLY: Hands up, and stop your squawking, sister.

ELSA: What's gotten into Mr. O'Reilly?

ROGER: He's not O'Reilly.

O'REILLY: I am Klaus Stansdorff of the Geheime Staatspolizei.

ELSA: The Gestapo!

O'REILLY: Temporarily assigned to the German Consulate in New York . . . as a cultural attaché.

KELLY: What's the Gestapo want with the Stage Door Slasher?

O'REILLY: What I want is for you, Sergeant Kelly, to take the lantern and lead the way into the closet.

KELLY: You can go to hell.

O'REILLY: *Bitte*, Sergeant Kelly. I could easily have killed you before but I didn't. Why not? Professional courtesy. Take the lantern.

KELLY: No.

O'REILLY: I suggest the rest of you turn your heads, as the bullet from this gun makes quite a large hole.

(As O'REILLY *levels gun at* KELLY, NIKKI *comes from door and puts a revolver at* O'REILLY*'s head.)*

NIKKI: Don't make a move, Daddio, or you'll be pushin' up daisies. *(She flashes I.D.)* Ensign Nicole Crandall, United States Naval Intelligence!

KELLY: *(Takes gun away from* O'REILLY*)* We're gonna need some rope.

ELSA: In the pantry. I'll get it. *(Exits)*

KEN: Someone go with her. She shouldn't be alone. *(Exits)*

ROGER: Wait, I'm not staying here with all these guns waving around. Bernice?

BERNICE: *(From desk, where she is writing)* Scotch and soda.

ROGER: Oh, never mind. *(Exits)*

NIKKI: Up against the piano, krauthead!

*(*NIKKI *has* O'REILLY *spreadeagled against the piano and is frisking him)*

EDDIE: Hey, where'd you learn to do that?

NIKKI: Basic training.

EDDIE: That's pretty basic, all right.

KELLY: *(Moves* O'REILLY *up against up right bookcase)* Okay, Ensign, I'll take over.

EDDIE: Naval Intelligence, I'll be damned!

NIKKI: We've been after this guy for three weeks.

EDDIE: No wonder you were always walkin' into tunnels. You were packin' a heater in your handbag.

KELLY: This cat a spy or something?

NIKKI: Worse, he's a saboteur. His name is Dieter Wenzel.

O'REILLY: You have the wrong man.

NIKKI: Shut your trap!

EDDIE: Wenzel?

NIKKI: That's right, Helsa's brother.

EDDIE: What's he doing here?

NIKKI: The Nazis landed this guy and five others on Long Island three weeks ago. We caught four of them in Sag Harbor posing as novelists.

O'REILLY: My name is Klaus Stansdorff.

NIKKI: Baloney. The saboteurs had false identities, a half million dollars, and a mission to blow up installations all over this country to effectively retard our nation's communications system.

EDDIE: Gee, I thought our post office was already takin' care of that.

NIKKI: But this guy and a guy named Franz Becker decided the money was more important than the Fatherland and took off with the do-re-mi.

EDDIE: So where's this guy's buddy, Becker?

NIKKI: The Katzenjammer Kid here bumped him off for the greenbacks. Right, Fritz?

O'REILLY: Wrong. I killed Becker because he was a traitor, dummkopf.

EDDIE: Hey, who you callin' dummkopf?

O'REILLY: Her I am calling dummkopf. You I call bumblenuts.

EDDIE: Just wanted to get that straight.

KELLY: So how'd you get on this guy's trail?

NIKKI: See, Naval Intelligence knew he had a sister. We figured it was a long shot, but he might head for her.

KELLY: They sent you alone against a killer?

NIKKI: I was the only agent who could sing soprano.

O'REILLY: Listen to me, all of you. Your lives are in great danger.

KELLY: Okay pal, we're all ears.

O'REILLY: I am not Dieter Wenzel. Dieter Wenzel is an officer in *Abwehr*—German military counterintelligence. He is also a homicidal maniac.

EDDIE: A homicidal maniac? How'd he get in the German army?

O'REILLY: We recruited him.

KELLY: And he's doing all the killing?

O'REILLY: Of course.

EDDIE: And where is he?

O'REILLY: He is . . .

(His eyes go wide. ELSA *enters with a bundle of clothesline.)*

ELSA: All right, here's the rope. I'll tie him up, I'm very handy with half hitches.

(O'REILLY *staggers forward and falls dead across the desk where* BERNICE *sits. A dagger, through a book, is in the middle of his back.)*

BERNICE: *(Rises, crosses to sit in wing chair.)* That's it! It's gone. The lyric is gone and I'll never get it back!

NIKKI: He's dead!

KELLY: There's blood on these books. The knife came right through here.

EDDIE: *(Examining book on* O'REILLY'*s back)* Moby Dick! I don't see how a knife got through that. I couldn't even finish the first chapter.

(KEN *enters)*

KEN: *(Seeing* O'REILLY) My God!

NIKKI: He was stabbed through the bookcase.

KELLY: *(Examining bookcase)* This is about where I was grabbed.

ELSA: There's a panel there. You just push that copy of *Faust.*

(KELLY *pushes book. Panel opens.)*

EDDIE: Holy mackerel!

KELLY: I'm goin' in. *(Exits into passage)*

ELSA: No, Sergeant . . .

(But he is gone)

It's useless. That passage branches off into five others.

(ROGER *enters*)

ROGER: *(Seeing* O'REILLY) Oh my God!

EDDIE: He was killed through the bookcase and practically fell on Bernice.

ROGER: *(Going to her)* Oh, Bernice, are you alright?

BERNICE: I can't work in this environment, Roger. These people have no respect for an artist. It's casting swirls to pine.

(Beat)

I am very drunk. *(Sinks into chair)*

KELLY: *(Entering from up right panel)* No good. It splits off five different ways just inside. Look, we're gonna take things a step at a time. Now first, let's get this guy outside with the others. Couple of you give me a hand.

(EDDIE, KEN, *and* KELLY *begin dragging* O'REILLY *out.*)

ROGER: *(Has picked up notebook from desk)* It's a consonant substitution.

(All look at him)

Poor Bebe's book. Someone was trying to work out the code.

NIKKI: I was.

ROGER: I love codes. Like playing Bach. Bebe was substituting numerals for consonants on a triplet basis.

NIKKI: How's it work?

ROGER: Very simple. Look . . .

EDDIE: *(From hallway)* Can we stop by the hall closet? I want to pick up my earmuffs this time.

(Men carrying O'REILLY *are gone.* ELSA *throws rope into closet)*

ROGER: It's very, very, easy. Especially since she repeats number sets. This becomes . . . "a" . . . "p" . . . "p" . . . "1" . . . apples. Here it repeats . . . apples. This is . . . aah . . . corn. Here's oranges. Some sort of ongoing shopping list. Peppermint. Apples again.

NIKKI: Apples, oranges, corn, peppermint . . . ?

ROGER: What do you make of that?

ELSA: Well, it might be some sort of salad.

ROGER: Really? I would think the peppermint might tend to dominate.

ELSA: Not if it weren't allowed to stand too long.

NIKKI: Maybe the sweetness of the oranges might counteract . . .

BERNICE: Word substitutes!

NIKKI: Word substitutes! Of course. It's another code!

*(*HELSA *enters center)*

HELSA: Pardon me, *gnädige Frau,* but the beef is getting dry and . . .

ELSA: Helsa!   ROGER: My God!   NIKKI: Helsa!

HELSA: Now what?

NIKKI: *(Pulls gun out of purse)* Put your hands up!

HELSA: *(One arm shoots up in a Nazi salute, and she quickly puts other arm up to cover.)* What is wrong with you people?

ROGER: We know you're the Stage Door Slasher, Helsa!

ELSA: You threatened me with a butcher knife.

HELSA: *Ach,* when you opened the closet! *Nein.* In addition to keeping the dinner warm, I have been running through the tunnels trying to keep from being murdered by my homicidal maniac of a brother.

NIKKI: Dieter Wenzel?

HELSA: *Ja.* He came here seeking refuge, posing as an Irish tenor.

ELSA: Mr. O'Reilly!

HELSA: *Ja.*

ELSA: But he's dead. They're burying him in a snowdrift right now.

HELSA: I will look. *(Crosses to look out French doors.) Ja,* that is Dieter. Poor Dieter. He was a very famous entertainer in Berlin, you know. Now he lies in a snowdrift with strangers.

ELSA: Yes. I hope there isn't a sudden thaw. I don't know what the milkman would think.

NIKKI: He was trying to kill you earlier?

HELSA: *Ja,* he knew I would turn him in to the authorities. You shot him, did you?

NIKKI: He was stabbed through the bookcase.

HELSA: *Ach so?*

(With terror)

Mein Gott, the tunnels!

ELSA: What about them?

HELSA: There is something else in there. Something evil. I have brushed against it in the dark.

ROGER: Have you seen it?

HELSA: If it is human—it is all in black—with the smell of death. It is demonic—and it waits—for us all.

(Beat)

Should I put the cucumbers back on ice, *gnädige Frau?*

ELSA: Yes, I suppose so. (HELSA *leaves*) Something evil . . . I'm going for the sergeant. (ELSA *leaves*)

NIKKI: Did Helsa actually threaten you?

ROGER: Well . . . she held a knife. And then we slammed the door in her face.

NIKKI: She could be telling the truth then.

ROGER: If she is, I think we should get out of this house as quickly as possible, blizzard or no blizzard.

NIKKI: If she is, it makes it all the more important that we crack this code.

ROGER: What's it say about the night of the murder?

NIKKI: Picadilly, 1020, tutu, toe shoes, leo, corn. What's another word for corn?

(KELLY *enters, followed by* ELSA, KEN, *and* EDDIE)

KELLY: No, no, no . . .

ELSA: But I'm the only one with even the slightest knowledge of these passages. I have to go.

KELLY: It's too dangerous for a woman.

ELSA: Not with this!

(Producing a derringer from behind some books. They all disappear, either into the walls or behind furniture. BERNICE *is still down left)*

The derringer which General von Grossenknueten carried as the personal bodyguard to the Archduke Ferdinand.

KELLY: *(Off stage)* You know how to use that thing?

ELSA: Sergeant, I have shot the "O" out of every stop sign in Westchester County.

KELLY: That's good enough for me.

(They all return)

Okay, here's the plan . . .

NIKKI: Listen everyone, we've broken part of the code in Bebe's book. Here's what it says the night of the murder: Picadilly, 1020, tutu, toe shoes, leo, corn.

KELLY: Corn? What's corn?

ROGER: A word substitute, we think.

KELLY: You think? She was a dancer, wasn't she? Maybe she had corns. Okay, here's the plan. We go in from the three passages outa here—one gun to a passage. The fourth gun stays here in case the fiend, or whatever it is, comes outa the walls.

(To ELSA*)* You take that passage. *(Points down left)*

Eddie, you pulled me outa those tunnels pretty good. You take this . . . *(Handing him the Luger)* . . . and go in through there. *(Points up right)*

EDDIE: Hey, if this don't have a flag pops out and says "Bang," I don't know what to do with it.

(Beat)

Boy, I've played some tough rooms in my life, but this one takes the cake.

KELLY: Ensign, you stay here.

NIKKI: Aye, aye, sir. I want to keep working on this code anyway.

KELLY: *(To* ELSA*)* Is there any place the tunnels don't lead?

ELSA: The pantry.

KELLY: Fine. *(To* KEN, ROGER, *and* BERNICE*)* You three go into the pantry. That way you'll be safe.

ROGER: Safety is exactly what I had in mind.

KEN: C'mon, Bernice. We're moving on.

BERNICE: Oh, good. Anything open this late?

*(*ROGER, KEN, *and* BERNICE *exit)*

KELLY: All set? Let's go!

ELSA: Move carefully—it's a maze in there. *(Exits down left.* KELLY *exits into the revolve.)*

EDDIE: *(To* NIKKI) You gonna be okay?

NIKKI: Yeah. Are you gonna be okay?

EDDIE: I asked you first. *(Starts to exit up right and stops)* Hey, listen, if I'm not back in twenty-four hours, cancel my ad in *Variety.*

(He exits. NIKKI *is alone for several moments . . . she sits down on the piano bench with the notebook, her gun on the piano near her.* KEN *enters center.)*

KEN: Roger and Bernice are all tucked in . . . surrounded by frying pans. Let's hope they don't get into a fight over a lyric.

NIKKI: Shouldn't you stay with them?

KEN: I thought I should be here with you. You've got a job watching three secret passages at once.

NIKKI: Thanks.

KEN: Still working on that book?

NIKKI: These foods as word substitutes—I just can't figure them.

KEN: Another code. And locked in Bebe's head forever, I'm afraid.

NIKKI: *(Into book)* Yeah.

KEN: I must congratulate you, Ensign, on your performance.

*(*NIKKI *looks at him)*

As a chorus girl. Quite convincing. Very detailed. The appearance . . . the walk. The trip over the suitcase was an excellent choice.

NIKKI: Well, actually that was me.

KEN: Oh. And your language. "Swell"—so typically crass. The ring of pure banal truth.

NIKKI: Well, that was kinda me too. See, I was a—hopeful, you know, knockin' around on the Great White Way, before I joined the Navy.

KEN: I see.

(Beat)

Did you by chance audition for me?

NIKKI: I don't know, Mr. de la Maize. I went to so many auditions. Maybe one of them was for you. Let's see . . . did you direct . . .

KEN: I think I would have singled you out.

NIKKI: Oh, I doubt that.

KEN: As different from the rest.

NIKKI: Different?

KEN: You didn't see yourself as different from the tawdry, shopworn, self-involved, run-of-the-mill chorus girl?

NIKKI: Gee, no. I thought most of 'em were pretty nifty.

KEN: Nifty.

(The word pains him. He crosses to bookcases.)

The chase must be going badly. I'd expected to hear shots ringing from the walls by now.

NIKKI: Wait a minute, maybe I did audition for you. Did you direct *I Married an Angel?*

KEN: That was Josh Logan.

NIKKI: And, let's see . . . I tried out for *Boys from Syracuse* . . .

KEN: George Abbott.

NIKKI: *Sing Out the News, Who's Who* . . .

KEN: Charley Friedman, Leonard Sillman.

NIKKI: Who's who—people!

KEN: What?

NIKKI: People. She was substituting food for people. She was probably keeping appointments she didn't want anyone to know about.

KEN: Anyone being Elsa, naturally.

NIKKI: So . . . that night, it was "corn, Picadilly, 1020 . . ." Who was "corn"? Corn . . . corny . . . a comedian in the show maybe. What's another word for . . .

(KEN *is behind her with a razor at her throat, as she realizes what "corn" stands for.*)

Oh my God!

KEN: Philo Vance would have gotten it much sooner, my pretty. *(Takes her gun)* Now, you and I will take a "swell" trip. *(He is taking her to revolving bookcase.)*

ROGER: *(Entering)* Naturally Bernice needs another drink so I've been elected to—

(Sees KEN *and* NIKKI)

Oh my God!

KEN: Don't do anything foolish, Roger.

ROGER: I don't want to deal with this. I absolutely refuse to deal with this.

KEN: I suppose you think I'm crazy. Well, I'm not crazy!

ROGER: Ken, I have no intention of getting dragged into a psychological discussion with you. God knows, I'm not feeling secure enough myself to hear your problems.

(ELSA *enters from closet)*

ELSA: How silly, I must have turned left at the hot water heater.

(Sees KEN)

Ken, what are you doing? Don't tell me you are the Stage Door Slasher?

KEN: I am.

ELSA: I asked you not to tell me.

KEN: Put your gun on the piano, Elsa, and get over there.

(She does. BERNICE *enters.)*

BERNICE: Excuse me.

KEN: Bernice!

BERNICE: *(Seeing* KEN, *heading back out)* I have the wrong room.

KEN: Don't move. Over there!

ELSA: But why, Ken, why?

KEN: Why what?

ELSA: Why did you kill all those girls?

KEN: My mother was a great person.

ROGER: You had to ask.

KEN: A simple woman born of simple stock.

ROGER: Is this going to be a long story, Ken?

KEN: My father left her for a ballet dancer.

NIKKI: I knew it!

KEN: She was beautiful.

ELSA: The ballet dancer?

KEN: No, my mother! Beautiful.

BERNICE: Yeah? Well, if you think so much of her, when's the last time you called her?

KEN: Well, it's been a couple of months, sure, but I've—*(Catching himself)* What do you care, anyway? You're going to die. All of you. It just remains to determine how.

ROGER: Ken, I'm not putting on a tutu for anyone.

KEN: A fire! Of course! What could be more natural with so many lanterns burning. *(He pushes* NIKKI *to piano, to be with the others.)* This house burning to the ground will keep me warm enough till help comes, don't you think? *(Starts to "direct")* Roger, get up. Elsa, sit down. Bernice, put your hands on the piano. Act natural! Nice. Good composition. Reminiscent of the final scene from *Berlin Calling*, the picture I made with Paul Lukas . . .

ROGER: Oh for God's sake!

KEN: . . . Helmut Dantine, Conrad Veidt, George Couloris, Oscar Homolka, and Merle Oberon. A picture which I assume you have all seen, since you've seen everything else I've done that hasn't been released. Little matter, since you're all going to die. Now, let's see . . . what can I use to make the flames spread more quickly?

(EDDIE *steps out of down left bookcase and hits* KEN *with a bottle of Cognac.)*

EDDIE: Try Cognac!

(KEN *collapses on the floor)*

NIKKI: Eddie! Wow, just in the nick of time!

EDDIE: Well, I was no sooner in the tunnels when it hit me what Miss von Grossen . . . ah . . .

NIKKI: . . . knueten . . .

EDDIE: . . . said.

ELSA: What did I say?

EDDIE: It's a maze in here. And what's another word for corn? Maize. Ken de la Maize. So I been tryin' to find my way back ever since.

BERNICE: Excuse me, if you're done with that Cognac, could I borrow it?

ROGER: You've had enough to drink, Bernice.

BERNICE: We're not at your house now, Roger; you don't have to count.

ELSA: *(With some wonder)* Ken de la Maize, the Stage Door Slasher.

EDDIE: Sure. He killed those dancers and then ran to hide in the one place where his madness, his paranoia, and his murderous inhuman tendencies would never be noticed.

ELSA: Where was that?

EDDIE: Metro-Goldwyn-Mayer.

ELSA: Oh my, we'd best go find Sergeant Kelly and tell him the chase is over. He could be wandering around in there for hours. Eddie, will you go in from that way?

(She is heading for revolve and points EDDIE *to down left)*

Can you hold the fort, Ensign?

NIKKI: Sure. Is there any rope?

ELSA: In the closet. Bernice.

*(*ELSA *goes into up right panel.)*

BERNICE: Well, I guess with the killer caught, it's okay this time.

(She sets the Cognac on piano and opens closet. HELSA *stands there with knife.* BERNICE *faints.* HELSA *calmly closes door.)*

ROGER: I'm so tired of picking this one up off the floor. *(Looks at her)* This calls for strong coffee.

NIKKI: Did she get the rope?

ROGER: What?

NIKKI: The rope.

(HELSA *opens closet door and tosses out rope . . . then closes door.*)

ROGER: *(Seeing rope)* Oh yes, here it is. *(Exits.)*

EDDIE: *(Picks up rope and brings it to* NIKKI) Listen, I really prefer being a comic to being a hero because when you're a hero you spend most of your time bein' scared out of your wits. But I better go back in those walls and tell Kelly we caught the Slasher.

NIKKI: And the saboteur.

EDDIE: *(Joking)* Yeah, but what about the sister who sells sausage? *(Both laugh)* Okay, I'll be right back. Maybe you should put another knot in that.

(EDDIE *exits into tunnel down left.* NIKKI *continues to tie* KEN. BERNICE, *on floor, sits up.*)

BERNICE: Where is everybody?

(HELSA, *carrying a small bag and a large knife, steps out of closet.* BERNICE *sees her and faints again.* HELSA *sets bag down, closes doors, and quietly moves to* NIKKI.)

NIKKI: Wait a minute . . . if Ken is the Stage Door Slasher, then who killed—

HELSA: I did.

(NIKKI *stands up*)

Be quiet. Don't scream and you may not get hurt. I know you have a gun and identification as an intelligence officer. Where are they?

(NIKKI *shifts weight as if getting ready to leap.* HELSA *laughs.*)

I also know what you are thinking. You are thinking . . . "This woman is smaller and I am trained in hand-to-hand combat. I can probably take that knife away from another, smaller woman."

(Removes wig)

But can you from a man?

NIKKI: My gosh! *(Glances at her handbag)*

HELSA: *Ach,* the handbag!

(They both lunge for bag. HELSA *slaps* NIKKI *and sends her flying down to the floor.* HELSA *takes gun and I.D. from bag.)*

If your naval intelligence was even a little intelligent, they would know that Dieter Wenzel was once the toast of the Berlin cabarets. Even more famous than Sally Bowles!

NIKKI: A female impersonator?

HELSA: The best. I do Lotte Lenya, Josephine Baker, and a great Dietrich.

(Sits on piano bench, one knee up, in famous Dietrich pose and sings a Dietrich song.)

(During song, BERNICE *has sat up, heard, and fainted again.)*

Also, my legs are better.

NIKKI: Then you killed . . .

HELSA: Everyone!

NIKKI: Miss Baverstock?

HELSA: I thought it was Fräulein von Grossenknueten. She had been sitting in that chair. With her out of the way, this house would have been mine. I also wanted people to think the Slasher was here, and it turned out, he actually was. I also killed the Gestapo agent.

NIKKI: Oh, really?

HELSA: No, O'Reilly. *(Laughs)* Just a little joke from the cabaret days. O'Reilly was, as he told you, Klaus Stansdorff. When Franz and I took off with the Fatherland's money, Franz hid in New York with his share. Stansdorff found him and killed him. Stansdorff must have also had information about my sister, so he came here.

NIKKI: Then it was your sister—

HELSA: Twin sister, *ja.*

NIKKI: You killed your own sister?

HELSA: We were never close. And I needed her identity. As I now need yours.

NIKKI: You'll never get away with this.

HELSA: Of course I will get away. I have a quarter of a million dollars and this is America!

NIKKI: How do you know so much about what went on—you weren't . . .

HELSA: The walls have eyes as well as ears, Miss Super Spy. *(Laughs)* If all Americans are as simple-minded as you, your capitol will one day be Berlin.

(HELSA *has tied* NIKKI's *hands, and has stood her up.)*

And now, Miss Naval Intelligence, you are about to disappear forever in the walls of this ridiculous house.

(EDDIE *enters out of panel down left. He is pointing a gun at* HELSA.)

EDDIE: Don't move! *(His hand starts to shake)* Stand still! I warn you, I'm a skilled marksman.

HELSA: *(Calmly takes gun out of his hand.)* The safety is on, Mr. Lone Ranger. *(Looking at gun)* A Luger. German gun. The best. Over there—next to her.

EDDIE: *(Crossing to* NIKKI) What happened to her hair?

NIKKI: She's a guy.

EDDIE: How come he's wearing a dress? Oh, I get it. *(To* HELSA) You're trying to dodge the draft.

HELSA: Very interesting country, America. Where else could you find a super spy and a comedian in one room?

EDDIE: The White House probably.

HELSA: All right, you two half-wits will now go into the tunnels.

EDDIE: What's he so burned up about, anyhow? You ask him to do the windows or something?

NIKKI: This is Dieter Wenzel.

EDDIE: The homicidal maniac? We could be in a lot of trouble.

HELSA: I am going to kill you.

EDDIE: Well, see, that won't be easy.

HELSA: Why not?

EDDIE: Because I'm scared of guns. So when they handed me that gun and asked me to run around in a dark tunnel with it, naturally I removed the bullets.

(HELSA *looks at gun.* EDDIE *hits her on head with Cognac bottle that* BERNICE *has left on the piano.*)

This Cognac really packs a punch.

NIKKI: Eddie, you're in the nick of time a second time.

(BERNICE *sits up, takes Cognac from* EDDIE.)

EDDIE: You tie up her—him—them—and I'll keep an eye on him. *(Crosses to* KEN. *Up right panel slides open and* KELLY *enters with gun.)*

KELLY: Don't anybody move!

EDDIE: It's okay, Sarge, we've caught the killers.

KELLY: *(Holding gun on* BERNICE) This is the Stage Door Slasher?

BERNICE: No, I'm the lyricist.

EDDIE: Over here, Sarge.

ROGER: *(Off)* Hello! Hello! Are you all right?

EDDIE: *(Pointing to* KEN) This is the Stage Door Slasher.

(BERNICE *unlocks door, letting* ROGER *in.* ELSA *enters from up right bookcase.*)

NIKKI: Helsa is a Nazi saboteur.

ELSA: Helsa a saboteur?

NIKKI: Only it's not Helsa. It's her brother Dieter. A female impersonator.

HELSA: I do Dietrich, Lotte Lenya, Josephine Baker . . .

ROGER: Really. Do you do Judy Garland?

HELSA: No, her voice is too rangy for me.

ROGER: Really, I would have thought if you did Lotte Lenya . . .

HELSA: Well, Lenya's is basically a chest voice, while Garland . . .

NIKKI: Yes, it's true, Garland is all head tones . . .

KELLY: Could we leave the musical discussion for another day? I wanna lock these two up.

KEN: I warn you, I have connections in very high places. I know Harry Cohen and Jack Warner personally. I have lunch with Louella Parsons.

KELLY: C'mon, you.

KEN: I have friends in Hollywood who are destined for political greatness. Unknown actors today, but someday . . .

KELLY: Fine, fine, when they come into office they can appoint you to their cabinet.

KEN: They will! They will!

(HELSA *does a Sophie Tucker imitation.*)

KELLY: Okay pal, save that for Sing-Sing.

HELSA: I will! I will! (KELLY *drags both of them out*)

EDDIE: Gee, we captured the Stage Door Slasher and a saboteur. We'll probably make Winchell.

(*Lights and radio on.* ROGER *turns radio off.*)

ELSA: We are restored to the world. I think the success of our adventure calls for a celebration. Let's repair to the dining room for Crêpes Flambées von Grossenknueten.

ROGER: Crêpes Flambées von Grossenknueten? Translated, that means sit very close to the fire extinguisher.

BERNICE: Corn, of course. Corn. That's it, Roger.

ROGER: What's it?

BERNICE: We're wrong setting our show in Washington. These are troubled times . . . times for a musical that celebrates the spirit of America. The cornfields, the cowboys, those surreys with all that frilly little crap on top. Our next musical should take place in . . . Nebraska.

ROGER: *(Singing)* N . . . E . . . B . . . R . . . A . . . S . . . K . . . A . . . Yow!

(ROGER *and* BERNICE *exit*)

ELSA: Well, you two performed quite heroically. The Navy will be proud of you, Nicole. I intend to write Eleanor about you. As for you, Mr. McCuen, I'm sorry this was not a real audition, or you certainly would have gotten the part. *(She exits)*

NIKKI: That's okay. He got the girl.

EDDIE: He did? I mean, I did?

NIKKI: Hey, how can I resist a guy who comes flyin' outa walls every time I need him?

EDDIE: I gotta warn you, I'm not a hero naturally.

NIKKI: No one's a hero naturally. Anyhow I'm not concerned about heroics. I'm concerned about chemistry.

EDDIE: That I got covered.

NIKKI: Yeah, I know—you inherited it.

(EDDIE *moves to kiss her. The French doors fly open and a young woman enters. She looks exactly like* HELSA *except her hair is in braids.*)

KATERINA: *Ach,* what a storm.

EDDIE: Helsa?

KATERINA: *Nein,* I am her cousin Katerina, from Coblenz, now living in Croton. I cook, clean, and keep house for Fräulein von Grossenknueten.

(EDDIE *and* NIKKI *laugh and fall into each other's arms as . . . the curtain falls.*)